# Theologizing en Espanglish

## STUDIES IN LATINO/A CATHOLICISM

*A series sponsored by the
Center for the Study of Latino/a Catholicism
University of San Diego*

*Previously published*

Orlando O. Espín and Miguel H. Díaz, editors, *From the Heart of Our People: Latino/a Explorations in Catholic Systematic Theology*

Raúl Gómez-Ruiz, *Mozarabs, Hispanics, and the Cross*

Orlando O. Espín and Gary Macy, editors, *Futuring Our Past: Explorations in the Theology of Tradition*

María Pilar Aquino and Maria José Rosado-Nunes, editors, *Feminist Intercultural Theology: Latina Explorations for a Just World*

Néstor Medina, *Mestizaje: (Re)Mapping Race, Culture, and Faith in Latina/o Catholicism*

# Theologizing en Espanglish

## Context, Community, and Ministry

*Carmen Nanko-Fernández*

ORBIS BOOKS

Maryknoll, New York 10545

Founded in 1970, Orbis Books endeavors to publish works that enlighten the mind, nourish the spirit, and challenge the conscience. The publishing arm of the Maryknoll Fathers and Brothers, Orbis seeks to explore the global dimensions of the Christian faith and mission, to invite dialogue with diverse cultures and religious traditions, and to serve the cause of reconciliation and peace. The books published reflect the views of their authors and do not represent the official position of the Maryknoll Society. To learn more about Maryknoll and Orbis Books, please visit our website at www.maryknollsociety.org.

Copyright © 2010 by Carmen Nanko-Fernández.

Published by Orbis Books, Maryknoll, NY 10545-0302.

Manufactured in the United States of America.

### Library of Congress Cataloging-in-Publication Data

Nanko, Carmen.
    Theologizing en Espanglish : context, community, and ministry / Carmen Nanko-Fernández.
        p. cm. — (Studies in Latino/a Catholicism series)
    Includes index.
    ISBN 978-1-57075-864-5 (pbk.)
    1. Church work with Hispanic Americans—Catholic Church. 2. Hispanic American theology. I. Title.
    BX1407.H55N36 2010
    230'.208968073—dc22

                                                          2009033221

two church boys
talking loud
on the train
praising the Lord
in espanglish hip-hop speak
—Willie Perdomo,
"The New Boogaloo"



Para toda mi familia, con cariño.
In memory of y en gratitud
para mis abuelos
Carmen y Emilio Fernández

# Contents

# Foreword

Who are these Latinos/as in our church and larger society? Or as Carmen Nanko-Fernández would spell it out, "Who are these Latin@s?

Identity has been a perennial issue for Latinos/as in the United States, particularly since every general identifier for this population has been coined by the dominant culture. Over the past twenty years, with few exceptions, every book on Latino/a theology has begun with a footnote by the author with his or her interpretation of and preference for *Hispanic* or *Latino,* recognizing that we Latino/as identify ourselves neither way.

Why has identity been so important to U.S. Latinos/as? Because personal agency begins with the ability to name oneself and so to define who one is in face of the other.

In this exciting volume of assorted essays, Carmen Nanko-Fernández takes on the identity issue from the inside. For her, Latino/a theologians have to be securely planted in their own sense of who they are. Otherwise our reflections are reactions to a world framed by the dominant group.

From the beginning Carmen sets out the raw statistics of the presence of Latino/as in the Catholic Church and in U.S. society, which set the context for articulating an identity from the inside. She critiques the attempts made to subsume the heart of Latino/a identity in the gray world of "diversity" and anchors the issue in *lo cotidiano,* the daily life of Latino/as.

It's *lo cotidiano,* according to Carmen, that creates the particularity of Latino/a identity and, therefore, of Latino/a theology. But it does so by affirming, rather than compromising, the particularity of others whose daily living is differently experienced and interpreted. By holding fast to a non-generalizing and non-dominating particularity of life lived *latinamente,* she is able to look out from the inside.

This perspective allows her to offer a harsh critique of church leadership that, besides not being numerically representative of Latino/as in the pews, attempts to articulate for Latino/as who they are and what they need rather than empowering the Latino/a community to do that for itself.

She takes a broad swipe at the way U.S. church documents have domesticated the cry for a preferential option for the poor, which arose with such passion in Latin America in the 1970s with liberation theology. She clearly documents how the U.S. bishops and many U.S. theologians took the passion out of the cry not by responding to the challenges of massive poverty in Latin America and their inherent critique of U.S. consumerism, but by focusing their attention on the Vatican's response (particularly that of the Congregation for the Doctrine of the Faith). The resulting conversation moved the preferential option for the poor out of the concrete context of people's lives and placed it in the theoretical world of economic analysis.

Carmen aims her critiques not just at the larger church or society but at the Latino/a community itself. She challenges what for many Latino/a activists and theologians has become emblematic of Latino/a identity in the United States: speaking Spanish. *Lo cotidiano,* Carmen claims, is not lived by many Latino/as in Spanish or in English, but rather in Espanglish.

One of Carmen's most interesting moves in these essays is her insistence on using this notion of hybridity as a key to understanding Latino/a identity from the inside. She takes this position not primarily from post-colonial theory or from the current literature on multiple belongings, but from the theological understanding of God's own rich self-diversity as a communion of persons, different one from the other but together being one God. This allows her to affirm Latino/as as *Imago Dei,* but in a world in which each human and each human group is likewise God's image and likeness.

She plays out the concrete consequences of this stance in her very creative reflections on the "truth about age" controversy surrounding *béisbol* (particularly, the case of Danny Almonte) in the Dominican Republic where, given the poverty of the general population, baseball becomes a way up and out. Does that concrete *lo cotidiano dominicano* (*béisbol,* not baseball) allow for a different ethical interpretation of the "truth about age" controversy than might be given from the perspective of daily life in the United States?

This fundamental unity in difference, found inside U.S. Latino/a identity itself, and in our relationship to others in the larger society, prepares the ground for what is the ultimate goal of *Theologizing en Espanglish:* a call for "building coalitions across marginalized communities in order to secure justice."

Ultimately, as is clear from these essays, articulating Latino/a identity from the inside is not a matter of narcissistic navel-gazing, but rather a way of affirming self in order to affirm the other. And it is those two affirmations together that create the possibility of a world of brotherhood and sisterhood, of equality and justice.

—GARY RIEBE-ESTRELLA, S.V.D.
CATHOLIC THEOLOGICAL UNION
PRESIDENT, ACHTUS

# Acknowledgments

Coming from a community that privileges teología y pastoral de conjunto, I would be remiss if I did not begin by acknowledging all those individuals and communities that make this book possible. I am grateful to the Center for the Study of Latino/a Catholicism at the University of San Diego for including *Theologizing en Espanglish* in their celebrated series Studies in Latino/a Catholicism. The center's founding director, Orlando Espín, is the padrino of this project and a source of enthusiastic and unshakeable support. The commitment of Orbis Books to publishing theologies from Latino and Latina perspectives invites both personal and communal appreciation; mil gracias to Robert Ellsberg and Sue Perry for their ongoing accompaniment and confidence in our scholarship. Words cannot begin to thank appropriately Jean-Pierre Ruiz for his gracious generosity in editing the manuscript of this book to prepare it for publication. His wisdom, insights, and unwavering friendship were instrumental in seeing this project through to publication.

I am indebted to mi familia: to my first teachers—my mom, Carmen, and my dad, Charles, mi querida Nana y mi Tía Connie Fernández; to my first colleagues—my two sisters, Mary Louise Cardosa and Anita Reagan, and my brother, Chip Nanko; to those who expanded our familial horizons mis cuñad@s Robert Cardosa, Peter Reagan, and Karen Nanko, y mis sobrin@s Danielle and BC Cardosa, Alyssa and Jessica Nanko; to mi familia de córazon Ed and Joanne Dobransky. This book would not have been completed without their loving encouragement, not to mention Mom's words, and the concerted efforts of the word-processing relay team of Mary Louise, Danielle, and Anita.

At this time in U.S. history, when pursuing an education is a dream denied to many of our alternately documented young people, I remain grateful for the opportunities provided to me by my almae matres Santa Maria School and Cardinal Spellman High School in the Bronx and the Catholic University of America in Washington, DC.

I am grateful to the community of scholars, ministers, professionals, and students at the Catholic Theological Union for their collegiality, warm welcome, and critical engagement with my scholarship. I am particularly appreciative of the efforts of colleagues who offered ongoing encouragement with respect to this project, the members of our annual faculty seminars, and especially Steve Bevans, C. Vanessa White, Mark Schramm, Mary Frohlich, Robert Schreiter, Richard McCarron, Barbara Reid, Barbara Bowe, and Laurie Brink.

In order to survive as a theological migrant worker—who is forever from the Bronx but living in Washington DC and laboring in Chicago—like many dislocated Latin@s, I too am blessed with a family for the road. I remain inspired and sustained by mis compañer@s who enliven my theologizing en conjunto on a daily basis, in more ways than they will ever know. They include Gary Riebe-Estrella, Gilberto Cavazos-González, Miguel Díaz, Orlando Espín, Neomi DeAnda, Raúl Gómez-Ruiz, y Jean-Pierre Ruiz. In this cyber age, teología en conjunto lives online en la tierra Facebook. Gracias amig@s y familia for the input. Some in la cyber comunidad have already been named in other places, but the gratitude extends to Jeremy Cruz, Bobby Rivera, Jacqueline Hidalgo, Eli Valentin, Jonathan Tan, Elias Ortega, Eddie DeLeon, Jaime Bascuñan, José Irizarry, y Dan O'Connell.

To all the communities who have influenced mi vida cotidiana, ¡gracias! Your presence permeates these pages. Finally, in a profound way I am indebted to the Academy of Catholic Hispanic Theologians of the United States (ACHTUS), with that community of scholars, con ellos me siento en casa.

A number of the chapters in this book first appeared in other publications in earlier versions. While they have undergone significant revision, they appear here with the permission of the publications in which the earlier versions appeared. These are: "We Are Not Your Diversity, We Are the Church! Ecclesiological Reflections from the Marginalized Many," which first appeared in *Perspectivas* (Fall 2006): 81–107; "The *Imago Dei* in the Vernacular," which first appeared as "Theologizing en Espanglish: The *Imago Dei* in the Vernacular," *Journal of Hispanic/Latino Theology* (January 25, 2009); "Handing on Faith en su propia lengua," which originally appeared as "Language, Community and Identity" in *Handbook of Latina/o Theologies*, 265–75 (Copyright 2006 by Edwin David Aponte and Miguel A. De La Torre. Chalice Press. http://www.ChalicePress.com. Reprinted by permission); "¡Cuidado! The Church Who Cares and Pastoral Hostility," which first appeared in *New Theology Review* 19, no. 1 (February 2006): 24–33; "Elbows on the Table: The Complex Contexts of lo popular," which first appeared as "Elbows on the Table: Ethics of Doing Theology/A U.S. Hispanic Perspective," *Journal of Hispanic/Latino Theology* 10, no. 3 (February 2003): 52–77; "Beyond Hospitality: Implications of Im/migration for Teología y Pastoral de Conjunto," which first appeared in *Perspectivas* (Fall 2006): 51–62. "Justice Crosses the Border: The Preferential Option for the Poor in the United States" first appeared in *A Reader in Latina Feminist Theology: Religion and Justice*, edited by María Pilar Aquino, Daisy L. Machado, and Jeanette Rodríguez (Austin: University of Texas Press, 2002), 177–203. That chapter also appeared in German translation as "Die Gerechtigkeit überschreitet die Grenze. Die Option für die Armen in den Vereinigten Staaten," in *Glaube an der Grenze, Die US-amerikanische Latino-Theologie*, edited by Raúl Fornet-Betancourt (Freiburg in Breisgau: Herder, 2002), 152–79.

# Introduction

The present volume brings together nine essays developed over the past seven years. Some of the pieces, originally published in other venues, were revised in an effort to prevent the redundancy that is often inevitable in this genre. In a certain way the chapters are variations on a theme, exploring the implications of taking daily lived experience seriously as a locus theologicus.

In the United States las teologías latinas are theologies dreamed in Spanish, articulated in English, and lived in Spanglish. The title of this collection, *Theologizing en Espanglish: Context, Community, and Ministry,* conveys the creative tension of this complex, multidimensional reality. Latin@ theologies participate in that "irruption of contextuality" that characterizes the late twentieth and early twenty-first centuries.[1] The jarring admission that theologies emerge from within complex matrices of lived experiences refocuses attention on communities of interpretation and calls for reflection from embedded theologians. This volume is part of that stream of theologizing that arises from within Hispanic particularity and that challenges the shortsighted notion that such theologizing is meaningful only to that ethnic particularity whose concerns shape its agenda.

## LANGUAGE MATTERS

At the outset I want to be clear about several distinguishing traits of my usage of language that might otherwise be puzzling to readers. The text employs several conventions that reinforce the dynamic and fluid interactions characteristic of a perspective arising from a Hispanic theological hermeneutic. The interruptions they may cause in reading mirror the impact of the Hispanic presence in the U.S. church and society, inviting a deeper level of informed engagement.

First, my use of @ is intentional; it is discussed in more detail in Chapter 2. It conveniently combines the "o" and "a" into one character that is gender inclusive, a practice utilized by other scholars, particularly in culture studies. As the symbol for "at" (@) it intensifies the significance of social location for doing theology from Latin@ perspectives, that is, latinamente. The use of @ in electronic communication marks it as both contemporary and as a means of highlighting networks of connection, two aspects constitutive of the Latin@ presence in the United States Finally, I add the acute accent (@́) as a reminder of the fluidity of language, culture, and identity. This character is created by adding the "combining acute accent" after el arroba.

Second, words and expressions in Spanish are not italicized unless they appear as such in direct quotations. This indicates the interaction between Spanish and English in the daily lived experience of U.S. Latin@s. In keeping with the creative use of lingual hybridity, at times sentences include both languages. The words of José Irizarry best express my intent: "A shift of language codes can bring new vistas into what was before ordinary and taken for granted."[2] The role of language, including Spanglish, in the construction of identity and community is found in Chapter 5. Third, I deliberately use *Hispanic* and *Latin@* interchangeably throughout the volume, thoroughly cognizant of the contested etymology of these umbrella terms.

## NOTES ABOUT COMMUNITY

The seismic shift in the Catholic population calls attention to the ethnic/racial communities that are now poised to shape the foreseeable future of the U.S. church. The Hispanic presence is at once ancient yet new, a product of sixteenth-century Spanish colonial enterprises, nineteenth-century U.S. expansionism, and twenty-first century migrations. The complexity of this gente defies simple categorization, and this has implications not only for theology but for ministry as well. "Imprecision in posing the notion of Latino 'ethnicity,' with its characteristic inattention to particularities and exclusions,"[3] can only result in flawed one-size-fits-all constructions of Hispanic ministry. Such undifferentiated and uncritical approaches, no matter how well intentioned, betray assumptions that perceive intra-Latin@ differences as "one more condiment in the festive sancocho,"[4] and Latin@s as the spice in the national stew. This text does not intend to be complicit in homogenizing the diversity that is the Latin@ reality, nor does it assume a monolithic culture.

Some scholars refer to our scholarship as emerging theology. Compared to the apostolic roots of our Catholic inheritance from España and the religious traditions of our indigenous and African roots, estamos verdaderamente entre los jóvenes: Latin@ theologies are truly young![5] Yet, when viewed in the light of the rich history of Iberian Christian theologies, it becomes amply clear that our thinking emerges from within a rich historical tradition.

In 1493, during his second cross-Atlantic voyage, Cristóbal Colón trips on Borinquen, and as long as Puerto Rico falls under the U.S. neocolonial umbrella, the stream of Latin@ theologies passes through Puerto Rico and the Caribbean. From 1823–1848, Cuban exile Félix Varela ministered with and defended the rights of New York City's immigrant poor in the Irish barrio, placing the stream of Latin@ theologies concretely in solidarity with migrating and disenfranchised peoples. In 1848 the Treaty of Guadalupe Hidalgo forced Mexico to cede 55 percent of its post-independence territory to the United States. This Mexican land became seven southwestern states, thus ensuring that the stream of Latin@ theologies forever crosses contested borders. In 1988 a small group of Latin@ theologians founded the Academy of Catholic Hispanic Theologians of the United States (ACHTUS), in effect formalizing our visible presence in the greater scholarly community.[6]

## SOME NOTES ON METHOD

This volume deliberately links theology and pastoral ministry, recognizing the dynamic interconnections between teología en conjunto and pastoral en conjunto. In other words, the practice of Christian faith, the accompaniment that constitutes pastoral ministry, and the critical reflections that arise from within are inextricably intertwined. This occurs within the context of our daily living, a vida cotidiana that is multidimensional and therefore calls for interdisciplinary engagement by theologians and other scholars. The goal is convivencia, a living together as community that is predicated upon analysis of the complexity of that living with the hopes of living together justly and well. A strong stream of postcolonial theory and analysis flows through these pages, and I owe this influence on my scholarship primarily to Latin@ biblical scholars, specifically Fernando Segovia and Jean-Pierre Ruiz.

Chapter 1, "We Are Not Your Diversity, We Are the Church! Ecclesiological Reflections from the Marginalized Many," examines the implications of the population shift that is remaking the face of the contemporary Catholic Church. For Hispanics, the move from being a marginalized minority to a plurality encourages new ways of rethinking communal identity. This is necessary to avoid the homogenization implicit in multicultural paradigms. Chapter 2, "De-Colonizing Practical and Pastoral Theologies," unmasks presuppositions that ground pastoral and practical theologies. The understanding of the daily, lo cotidiano, by Latin@ theologians reconfigures the turn to experience. The complexity of la comunidad latina defies abstract constructions of liberation or simplistic constructions of identity. The postcolonial thread continues in Chapter 3, "Ortho-proxy and Orthopraxis: The Ethics of Right Representation." The ethical significance of agency and representation bears import on understandings of ecclesiology. Chapter 4, "The Imago Dei in the Vernacular," reconceptualizes representation as a matter for theological anthropology. Chapter 5, "Handing on Faith en su propia lengua," problematizes binary and bilingual imaginaries of community in dialogue with the experiences of Deaf Latin@s. From the ambivalent creation of linguistic diversity at Babel in Genesis 11:1–9 to the reception, "each in our own native language," of the Pentecost proclamation of "God's deeds of power" (Acts 2:1–11), language has been a source of theological reflection with important practical implications. The focus moves to pastoral care as a constitutive element of ministry in Chapter 6, "¡Cuidado! The Church Who Cares and Pastoral Hostility." Genuine caring in the setting of daily experience is manifest in commitments that attend to the interrelationship between personal needs and systemic injustice. At times this calls for prophetic responses captured in the expression hostilidad pastoral, that is, pastoral hostility.

Chapter 7, "Elbows on the Table: The Complex Contexts of lo popular," expands theological consideration of the popular beyond the confines of the narrowly religious. The chapter explores the intersections of la vida cotidiana and globalization through the lens of béisbol. The theme of migrations, which emerges in the previous chapter, continues in "Beyond Hospitality: Implications of (Im)migration for Teología y Pastoral de Conjunto." Chapter 8 situates migrations in the context of real people and proposes trajectories mindful of the complexity of the situation. Chapter 9, "Justice Crosses the Border: The Preferential Option for the Poor in the United States," is consistent thematically in its concern for social justice. It traces the entrance of the option for the poor into U.S. ecclesial discourse and evaluates its particular reception within that context.

The arrangement of the book's chapters in this way draws attention to communities, spaces, and places that indicate different ways of being that are not always accounted for in the theological academy or even in pastoral ministry. In some ways these chapters as configured in this book offer what amounts to a "dissident cartography," a mapping proposal that juxtaposes experiences that might not normally appear in proximity to one another.[7] In that sense they interrupt the norm and offer opportunities to entertain new ways of theologizing, not only en Espanglish. Material in these pages that first appeared in print has been revised, very extensively in many cases. While individual readers of this book might profitably begin with any chapter, or pick and choose from among the chapters that might be of special interest, my suggestion that the whole book offers a "dissident cartography" invites readers to discern the threads that run through the argument of the whole book, even when, at first glance, Latin American béisbol, rappers from the Bronx, and the Imago Dei might appear to be unconventional juxtapositions.

Finally, in many venues and at many tables, this book itself developed as a matter of a very lively and sustained teología en conjunto. By no means is the publication of the book intended to close the circle or to bring that theologizing en conjunto to an end. It is my hope that readers of this book might themselves be prompted to engage in theologizing about context, community, and ministry, whether in Espanglish or in any other lengua cotidiana.

# We Are Not Your Diversity, We Are the Church!

## Ecclesiological Reflections from the Marginalized Many

A lone sheep cries out:
*There are more of us than them!*
The flock keeps grazing.

—MARTÍN ESPADA[1]

As a U.S. Hispanic Catholic theologian, I take comfort and find challenge in a description by Luis Rivera-Pagán of that proto-Latino theologian Bartolomé de las Casas: "His was the bitter honor of having many public noisy detractors and many secret silent admirers, ever since that day . . . in which he had the

An earlier version of this chapter appeared in *Perspectivas* (Fall 2006): 81–107. That version developed two different papers delivered at the 2003 and 2005 annual meetings of the Catholic Theological Society of America (CTSA). See Gary Riebe-Estrella, "The Vocation of the Latino/a Theologian: Speaking for Whom? Speaking to Whom?" *Proceedings of the Fifty-eighth Annual Convention of the Catholic Theological Society of America* 58 (2003), 147–48; Gary Riebe-Estrella, *Proceedings of the Sixtieth Annual Convention of the Catholic Theological Society of America* 60 (2005), 142–43.

enigmatic intuition of being called to a prophetic vocation."[2] I keep these words in mind because this chapter raises questions that need to be raised by theologians emerging from la comunidad latina in the U.S. Catholic Church, a community that can now best be described as a marginalized plurality. I resonate with Espada's prophetic sheep calling the flock not only to "do the math," but to explore the ethical implications of this nueva realidad.

"Doing the math" involves consideration of the statistics that provide insight into the Latin@ presence in the U.S. Catholic Church and the pastoral responses of the institutional leadership to this growing community. Attention to the context of this nueva realidad also entails examining the pastoral responses of the church in terms of the understanding of diversity that implicitly guides decisions affecting ministry with la comunidad latina. Theological reflection on diversity is necessary. Three loci—difference, commonality, and hybridity—emerge as distinct sources for such reflection.

## CONTEXTUAL HORIZONS

Orlando Espín reminds us that any theology of grace is dependent on the daily lived experience of the theologian and his or her local community;[3] in other words, our first ethical responsibility is to acknowledge and recognize that each of our vidas cotidianas influence our individual methodologies, foundations, and starting points for reflection. "*Lo cotidiano* makes social location explicit for it is the context of the person in relation to physical space, ethnic space, social space."[4] Theologies that emerge from U.S. Latin@ perspectives have an integrity that is marked by openness to admit that our perspectives are situated and engaged. In other words, to do theology latinamente is to do so en conjunto.

Disembodied theologies result from failing to take into account the social contexts and lived experiences that shape our

theological lenses as well as those of our colleagues and predecessors in the academy and in the church, and the communities
to whom we are accountable. To take this impact seriously does
not mean we make our stories normative, but it does challenge
temptations to universalize particular theologians or schools of
thought as though they somehow transcend particularity. In many
ways all theologies are contextual and to a degree autobiographical. Miguel Díaz reflects this in how he frames his conversation
with Karl Rahner, appropriately entitled *On Being Human: U.S.
Hispanic and Rahnerian Perspectives*. Díaz notes:

> My aim is to pave the way into an *analogical appreciation*
> of these two distinct but interrelated Catholic theological
> anthropologies, and their respective contexts. Whenever
> appropriate as a result of the ensuing conversation, chal-
> lenge and critique will be carried out from the contextual
> horizon of each conversational partner. In so doing, we hope
> to avoid falling into the error of what Raúl Fornet-
> Betancourt . . . has characterized as turning a specific cat-
> egorical world into the center and horizon by which other
> worlds are accepted and understood.[5]

What are the contextual horizons out of which U.S. Hispanic
Catholic theologians reflect and write? The numbers indicate
that the varied communities of people counted and included under
the politically and socially charged umbrella terms of *Hispanic*
and/or *Latino/a* constitute the fastest-growing minority in the
United States and the largest community in the U.S. Catholic
Church. According to the figures provided by the United States
Conference of Catholic Bishops (USCCB), approximately 39 percent, or 25 million, of the nation's 67.3 million U.S. Catholics
are Hispanic.[6] Nationally, as well as in the Catholic Church, the
Latin@ population is characterized by its relative youth, with
Hispanics making up 41 percent of all Catholics under the age
of thirty, and 44 percent of children under the age of ten.[7]

Seventy-one percent of U.S. Catholic population growth since 1960 is attributed to la comunidad latina.[8] But the numbers of Catholic Hispanic theologians have not kept pace proportionately with this reality, and the face of ecclesial leadership fails to reflect what is not only the future of the church but its present. Currently, less than 10 percent of U.S. Catholic bishops are Latinos. There is a ratio of one bishop to every 231,000 Catholics in the United States but only one Hispanic bishop to every one million Latino/a Catholics in the country.[9] To date there has not been a U.S. Hispanic cardinal. In 2009, 13 percent of the men ordained for diocesan priesthood and 9 percent for religious institutes were identified as Hispanic/Latino.[10] In seminaries, "whites still account for nearly two thirds of priesthood candidates enrolled in theologates. One in six (15 percent) is Hispanic/Latino."[11]

At the grassroots level limited financial resources and lower levels of educational attainment affect the number of Latin@ laity involved in ecclesial ministries that do not require ordination. For example, Latin@s make up approximately 12 percent of participants in lay ecclesial ministry programs nationwide; in comparison, "nearly eight in ten participants . . . are white. . . . Hispanics/Latinos are much less likely to be enrolled in degree programs in lay ecclesial ministry formation and whites are much more likely to be enrolled in degree programs. Hispanics/Latinos are 6 percent of students enrolled in degree programs and 10 percent of students enrolled in certificate programs."[12] It is also telling that Latin@s are "more likely to be providing their ministry as unpaid volunteers (25 percent compared to 12 percent)."[13]

The obvious implications of under-representation in all forms of ecclesial leadership is that more often than not Latin@ programs, parishes, and offices on the local and diocesan levels are managed by non-Hispanics; the presence of Latin@s in leadership, outside of the sphere of Hispanic ministries, is minimal. The correlation between under-representation and educational attainment cannot be overstated. The U.S. bishops themselves admit that "the limitation of resources dedicated to the education of Latinos has a direct impact on the number of Hispanics who have the necessary credentials to hold leadership-level positions."[14]

Not only are Latin@s undereducated for ministerial leadership, but even fewer are involved in the education and formation of the church's ministers. According to the data collected by the Association of Theological Schools (ATS) from its member institutions, the presence of Latin@s as students and faculty in theological education hovers around 3 percent. Latin@s remain the most under-represented community in the academy, especially in light of the size and exponential growth of the Hispanic population in general.[15] The fall 2008 degree-completion numbers for doctoral-level programs at ATS schools are not encouraging: four men and three women earned the Ph.D./Th.D., and thirty-five men and two women the doctor of ministry degree.[16] These numbers are not specific with regard to denomination, so for Catholics the future appears particularly bleak. This minimal presence is reflected in a breakdown of the doctoral fellowship recipients of the Hispanic Theological Initiative from 1997 to 2005.[17] Statistics indicate that 62 percent percent of the eighty-two awardees were Protestant and 38 percent were Catholic, a group that "does not mirror the religious orientation of Latinos in the general population."[18]

The human resource problem is coupled with a lack of material resources. Numbers alone do not necessarily translate into influence or access to those with decision-making or decision-breaking power. The Hispanic population in the church may have grown exponentially, but low representation in ministerial leadership and a paucity of presence in the education and formation of scholars and ministers give rise to skepticism about the institutional church's commitment to ministry with la comunidad latina. For example, the closures and/or mergers of parishes and schools across the nation have hit African Americans and Latin@s particularly hard. Commenting on school closings that would disproportionately affect poor and working-class neighborhoods in his archdiocese (Chicago), Cardinal Francis George noted,

"While the commitment remains strong, the resources remain limited."[19]

Meanwhile, in the Archdiocese of Washington, the Hispanic population has quadrupled over the past twenty-five years; Latin@s now constitute at least 40 percent of the Catholic community there. In response, a pastoral plan several years in the making was released in June 2006. Entitled *Diverse in Culture, United in Faith*, the five-year plan is to be funded out of the archdiocesan capital campaign, so that implementation will require no "shifting of priorities and resources at the expense of other ministries."[20]

Clearly this remains to be seen, but as demonstrated with the situation in Chicago, there remains a disconnect between commitment to la comunidad latina and the recognition that this entails a serious allocation and reprioritization of both human and material resources. If not, Hispanic Catholics risk rapidly becoming a marginalized majority in our own church. It is worth heeding the experience of one parish lay leader: "I am discouraged by the fact that we, Hispanics, don't count here in this parish. We come to mass in great numbers and our Masses are really filled with the spirit. But all the power is in the hands of a small group of (non-Hispanic) old-timers who contribute a lot of money to the Church."[21]

## DEALING WITH DIVERSITY: HOMOGENIZING DIFFERENCE

The sense of disempowerment is not only a local experience, but it is communicated in an understanding of diversity that implicitly guides the direction of Hispanic ministry decisions by the ecclesial leadership. Two national examples from the USCCB, *Encuentro 2000* and the 2006 proposal for the creation of a committee on culturally diverse communities, illustrate the marginalization that results for the U.S. church's largest population when ecclesial leaders interpret diversity as difference that must be controlled.

In 1997 the U.S. bishops accepted the recommendation of the Hispanic Affairs Committee to "convoke a national gathering in the Jubilee Year 2000 to celebrate the rich cultural diversity of the Church in the United States."[22] In the words of Bishop Gerald R. Barnes, then chairman of the Bishops' Committee on Hispanic Affairs, the premise of this fourth Encuentro was that the past three Encuentros had "given them [Hispanics] an opportunity to pray and share and listen to and with one another. As we begin the Third Millennium of Christianity, Hispanic Catholics in the United States want to gather once again with all their brothers and sisters in the Church to celebrate the cultural richness of the Catholic faith and to plan for new ways of evangelizing."[23] Portrayed by the Bishops' Conference as "a response to the challenges of serving culturally diverse communities, and especially the Hispanic community,"[24] this national intercultural event was convened in July 2000 in Los Angeles, California.

> The Committee on Hispanic Affairs and Hispanic Catholics served as the hosts and lead agents of Encuentro 2000: Many Faces in God's House . . . [which] marked the first time that the Church in the United States gathered to recognize, affirm, and celebrate the cultural and racial diversity of its members. With the participation of more than five thousand leaders representing the many faces of the Church . . . Encuentro 2000 inspired and challenged Catholics in the United States to embrace a Catholic vision for the third millennium in which all are welcomed to the Father's table.[25]

This event was not unaccompanied by controversy. There had been a degree of ownership by Hispanic Catholics of the Encuentro name and process that was nurtured over three national meetings from 1972 to 1985. Encuentro was a way of meeting, developed with Catholic Latin@s, that promoted agency, favored consultation, and served as a means to involve the grassroots in the ecclesial decisions that affected la comunidad. While the initial idea of a more inclusive Encuentro recognizing the variety of cultures in the U.S. church was said to have come from the Hispanic Affairs Committee, there was a sense, on the part of some, that the name, process, and players had been coopted. The positive spin on Encuentro 2000 was that it reflected the hospitality of the new plurality in recognizing "the many faces in God's house." The reality was that this invitation had come from the bishops of the United States, and the faces of those with the power to extend the invitation did not (and do not) reflect this rising majority.

Conspiracy-minded observers might wonder how and why a process developed with Latin@s struggling for their due attention in the church was transformed into a polycultural invitation to all. Why was such an invitation unfathomable when other ethnic groups constituted the dominant population? Why was it now so important to provide

> an opportunity for the Church in the United States to gather, to engage in profound conversations about life and faith, to worship together, to learn from each other, to forgive one another and be reconciled, to acknowledge our unique histories, and to discover ways in which we, as Catholic communities, can be one Church yet come from diverse cultures and ethnicities.[26]

Why did the Encuentro, a gathering and process for empowering a particular disenfranchised community, suddenly have its focus change to "hospitality and strengthening the unity of the Church in a cultural context."[27] What had changed? The demographics! The words of Fernando Segovia are eerily applicable here:

> In a sense the debate is no longer on the question of access but rather on the question of critical mass—how many is

too many? Even in the most liberal of settings, there is this
lurking fear of "the other," those not like us, especially when
the possibility of a critical mass begins to come into play.
Again, the question of a numbers ceiling is crucial: a critical mass must be avoided at all cost; it is the only way of
providing access while holding on to power. . . . A critical
mass is impossible to control.[28]

The operational understanding of diversity and the resulting
marginalization are also evident in the restructuring of the national conference. At their June 2006 meeting the U.S. bishops
entertained a proposal that would consolidate and/or eliminate
a number of standing committees. Among the cuts included in
this plan was the Hispanic Affairs Committee. The office that
supported this committee was significantly understaffed in pro-
portion to the Latin@ presence in the church, and under the
new configuration Hispanic Affairs would take its place under a
multicultural umbrella.

A Committee on Culturally Diverse Communities would
replace current standing committees on African-American
Catholics and Hispanic affairs and the ad hoc committee
dealing with Native American Catholics. That committee
would also be responsible for Catholics of Asian and Pacific Island descent, for which there is no current committee. It would have responsibility over the pastoral care of
migrants, refugees and people on the move, which is currently under the aegis of the migration committee.[29]

At the time, concerns were raised that creating a "Diverse
Culture Committee that would include all ethnic and racial groups
would perhaps diminish the need to focus even more on pastoral
outreach to the Hispanic Community, which is such a large and
growing community."[30] This was not new. In 2001 a group of
regional and national leaders in Hispanic ministry, convened by
the Hispanic Affairs Committee of the USCCB, identified a set

of challenges facing the ongoing development of ministry with la comunidad latina. The group expressed reservations about "multicultural" models that would consolidate minorities under one umbrella, thus diluting the particular identities and visions of the absorbed ethnic ministries. Concerns were raised about a reduction of resources, limited access to bishops, exclusion of the Hispanic ministry staff from pertinent decision-making processes and the overall effect on the church's ministries and mission.[31] In retrospect, the ambivalent response of the bishops appears to have anticipated the subsequent restructuring proposal: "We bishops are mindful of the cultural diversity of the Church and of the need for effective ministry models. However, the size and long-standing presence of the Hispanic population call for an assertive response by the Church to the challenge of ministering among Hispanic Catholics."[32]

Both Encuentro 2000 and the proposed restructuring plan are indicative of the bishops' understanding of diversity. These two cases reflect an implicit attitude whereby difference is problematized, though euphemistically referred to as challenge. Diversity is not conceived of as a shared human and ecclesial condition; rather, it is a way of referring to the ever-increasing presence of so-called minorities and immigrant populations. Diversity is in contrast to an unspoken normative understanding of the U.S. church, characterized as Anglophone and assimilated immigrant. The differences of generations of immigrants, primarily from across Europe, and the pastoral challenges that accompanied their linguistic, cultural, economic, racial, and ethnic particularities are homogenized and romanticized at best, forgotten at worst. "English only" was used against Slavic peoples; "whites only" discriminated against countless Mediterranean peoples; "Irish need not apply" restricted access to economic and social mobility. These communities too are the diversity of the church, yet they are absent from the proposed Diverse Culture Committee. The African American, Hispanic, and Native American communities predate the majority of the European presence in the United States; these communities are not the "new" face of the church. Yet somehow they qualify for the Diverse Culture Committee. La comunidad latina is the largest presence in the church. Should it not be the norm and all others fall under the purview of the umbrella group? In light of the Hispanic plurality, should not the descendants of earlier waves of immigration—English, Irish, Italian Polish, German—now be considered the diversity?

Both Encuentro 2000 and the proposed Diverse Culture Committee expose the operative paradigm: diversity is synonymous with difference and needs to be controlled. Difference suggests under-representation in leadership, vulnerability, need—especially with regard to social services, dislocation, and a degree of powerlessness, usually imposed from without though not recognized as such. The pastoral responses that accommodate this understanding of diversity amount to token gestures. To borrow the words of Justo González, the church

> can set up an office for "ethnic minority issues"; it can develop a "national plan for Hispanic ministry" and then keep it marginal to the rest of the church; it can "elevate" a few token minorities to positions of bureaucratic responsibility. . . . The church can find a dozen ways to tell ethnic minorities as well as other marginalized people that they are welcome in the church, but that their presence is a problem.[33]

As theologians, what are the questions that we need to entertain in light of this nueva realidad? The overwhelming and growing presence of Latin@s in the U.S. Catholic Church and the pastoral responses of current ecclesial leadership invite us as Hispanic theologians to explore diversity latinamente. Diversity discourse is not neutral, and its presuppositions have practical implications and pastoral consequences. The church's shifting contextual horizon challenges paradigms that confuse universality with a powerful normative particularity. Theological reflection needs first to examine three loci that serve as sources for

contemporary conversation and scholarship on diversity: difference, commonality, hybridity.

## DIVERSITY THROUGH THE LENS OF DIFFERENCE

Difference as a starting point for theological reflection on identity and diversity has both advantages and limitations. The celebration of difference and a valuing of particularity is not a matter
of political correctness or simply "identity politics." Rather, it is
a way of responding to centuries of equating alterity as inferior-
ity, a means of addressing systemic injustices and unequal access
by promoting identity-based agency. Focusing on difference provides space for personal and collective identities to emerge and
assume a visible public presence in una tierra that prizes assimilation. From *e pluribus unum* to the body of Christ, accommo-
dating difference within community remains a concern in the
construction of identity.

A focus on difference is not without its limitations. Exclusive
constructions of difference too often miss intertwined legacies
and multiple belongings. For example, a number of famous con-
tributors who are commemorated during Hispanic Heritage
Month (September/October) also grace our celebrations of African American Heritage Month (February). These include the
Afroborinqueño Arturo Alfonso Schomburg, curator of the largest collection of African and African American cultural materials in the world; Eugene Marino, first African American Catholic archbishop in the United States, son of a Puerto Rican father;
Martin de Porres, first black saint of the Americas; and the Negro League's New York Cubans baseball team.

Some Hispanic theologians have reflected on difference as locus theologicus and recognized its limitations, including the danger of reifying the very stereotypes we sought to counter. As María
Pilar Aquino reminds us, "Any theological discourse that takes
seriously into account the plural fabric of reality and of knowledge must deal also with the asymmetric character of social power

relations at all levels. Theological discourse must critically confront the ethnocentric tendencies of all cultures, including its own, as well as avoid romanticizing its notions of family, community and people."[34]

Difference alone, whether experienced as Fernando Segovia's being from two places but with no place to stand[35] or subsumed under umbrella terms like Latin@ or Hispanic, inadequately describes the experiences of communities and individuals whose diversity defies description. In *From Bomba to Hip Hop: Puerto Rican Culture and Latino Identity,* Juan Flores cautions against "generic, unqualified usage" of these terms. These categories can be employed to "mislead the public into thinking that all members and constituents of the composite are in basically the same position in society and all are progressing toward acceptance and self-advancement from the same starting line, and at the same pace. . . . Thus what presents itself as a category of inclusion and compatibility functions as a tool of exclusion and internal 'othering.'"[36]

Difference discourse further leads to exclusion when one considers that the postmodern absolutization of particularity and otherness still leaves the rules for engagement, the invitation to greater conversation, and the framework for dialogue in the hands of those who are considered dominant (but not necessarily constituting a majority). These perspectives of dominance tend to see only the particularity of others, not their own. By refusing to own their *own* difference, they confuse their particularity with universality. So when the so-called dominant permit the exotic, different, ethnic, alternate perspectives into the conversation, Roberto Goizueta observes we still remain "'true to the experience' of only those who share the particular perspective or social location."[37] Dismissed as "particular and other,"[38] and therefore deemed meaningful primarily to our own particular constituencies, alternate perspectives never necessarily need influence the greater conversations or be relevant to the experiences of more dominant, or assumed, normative perspectives. Fernando Segovia explains, "If the stress now falls on the dissimilarities, it is only because of the need to balance the long-standing modernist stress on commonalities, which in turn were ultimately defined by the dominant culture and thus exhibited an eerie resemblance to the particularities of that culture."[39]

## DIVERSITY THROUGH THE LENS OF COMMONALITY

James Nickoloff, addressing diversity from the perspective of gays and lesbians, seeks to "assert sameness from the side of, and on behalf of, those whom church and society scorn."[40] His appropriation of sameness as entry into identity/diversity discourse is not naive. It is, rather, a liberating act of resistance: "Along with other oppressed people, we have discovered that nothing causes greater offense than to tell those who despise us that in fact they and we are essentially the same."[41] Nickoloff posits "fundamental similitude" as a starting point for understanding diversity as "differentiated oneness" because he is concerned that "*beginning* with alterity or hybridity often means *staying with* alterity or hybridity, that is, keeping oneself at arm's length from the other."[42] This critique is valid because the difference and hybridity approaches risk ghettoizing their own constituencies and prevent solidarity across self-imposed barrios. In the long term, permanent classes of others and/or conditions of otherness prevent appreciation of a common creation in the image and likeness of the divine, a recognition of a common humanity that commands us to love our neighbors as ourselves (Mt 12:31). This radical concept challenges us to recognize ourselves even in our enemies.

While I concur with Nickoloff's suggestion to proclaim "homotruth," in reality our humanity is reducible to a limited set of least common denominators. All humans have our origins outside of ourselves. All humans are embodied, as is our multiple belongingness. All humans die, and for some faith traditions, all humans are created in the divine image.

My uneasiness with sameness as a starting point is rooted in concern for the slippery slope from common to normative. Too often the common and the normative are confused as interchangeable. Who determines what is common and what are the implications of assumptions of commonality?

I am reminded of an email I received from a Deaf Korean I had accompanied through his master's of divinity thesis process.[43] Min Seo Park's hope for me was that I could be Deaf. This was not an infliction of a burden but a sincere desire for me to be normative. Though we could communicate effectively in sign language, parsing the nuances of theology, and while I was certainly in solidarity with Min Seo's ministry and the Deaf community, I do not know what it is to be deaf or to experience Deaf culture as an insider. This particular source of our commonality did not exist, though there was genuine solidarity across our differences.

Nickoloff rightly points to the power differentials present in declaring sameness; sameness in the hands of the powerful can become cooptation and not a source of liberation. Unfortunately, the assimilation discourse of people like Samuel Huntington also conceals the move from common to normative. I am skeptical of propositions with the potential to ignore, obfuscate, and minimize the contextuality of our individual and communal lives, ultimately leading to a blurring of identities that those of us in marginalized communities have struggled to articulate and get taken seriously in the academy, church, and society. Roberto Goizueta communicates well this frustration:

> At the very historical juncture when Latinos and Latinas are asserting our historical subjectivity and the value of our own experience as *locus theologicus*, we are now advised that the historical subject does not exist and that value is an arbitrary, artificial construct. At the very historical juncture when we are articulating and developing a theological language that will allow us to enter into "rational

discourse" with the church and academy, we are advised
that reason does not exist, only intuition, ambiguity, and
irrationality.[44]

The context for the construction and reconstruction of identity by Latin@s has changed dramatically in the past thirty years.
Statistics indicate that the time has come to redefine our understandings of ourselves as comunidad. One in seven people in the
United States is Hispanic. Immigration and higher birth rates
have made Latin@s the largest racial/ethnic minority community in the United States, and it is estimated that in the next few
decades Hispanics will constitute a quarter of the U.S. population. Since Latin@s are already the largest population in the U.S.
Catholic Church, it would not be in our best interests to pursue
commonality at the very time that the particularity of our Hispanic difference might well be the norm, especially when current
constructions of "common" lack any hint of sabor latino. How
does a once-minority community avoid becoming a marginalized
majority in its own church, or eventually in its own nation? In a
twist on assimilation, these demographic shifts may suggest what
Ed Morales calls the "contradiction of miscegenation as a potential solution"; in other words, that North America is beginning "its long-overdue process of assimilation into the greater
American hemisphere."[45]
Nickoloff's invitation to consider what makes us common is
necessary when one takes into account the damage done when
communities and nations isolate differences. The genocides of
the twentieth century should temper any naive appropriation of
identity politics. However, I have difficulty reconciling Nickoloff's
admirably nuanced handling of commonality in service to liberation with, for example, Samuel Huntington's frightening assimilation rhetoric. In the hands of Huntington, "the common"
is a desperate attempt to protect what is currently dominant before the difference becomes the dominant. For Huntington, the
demographics are a source of fear. He clearly establishes the criteria for U.S. commonality and for belonging, sadly the same

criteria employed to whitewash countless generations of immigrants whose rich diversity is reduced in the United States to festivals and food, fiestas y comidas. In the words of Huntington, "There is no Americano dream. There is only the American dream created by an Anglo-Protestant society. Mexican Americans will share in that dream and in that society only if they dream in English."[46]

## DIVERSITY THROUGH THE LENS OF HYBRIDITY

For a number of Latin@ theologians, reflecting on hybridity is a familiar and preferred entry point into identity/diversity discourse. Typically expressed in the language of mestizaje, and mestizaje/mulatez, these reflections attempt to deal with interculturality and the embodied-ness of our hybridity. As María Pilar Aquino suggests, "Precisely because *mestizaje* has been portrayed by dominant cultures as carrying a social value only worthy of exclusion, a *mestizo/a* theology will highlight the vital syntheses which 'new peoples' have interculturally created in order to explain their own vision and their own identities."[47] Aquino goes on to caution that a biological condition does not necessarily presume the development of intercultural consciousness.

Probably the most prominent and enduring metaphor in Hispanic theological discourse on diversity, mestizaje and the resulting new creation adds another dimension to constructions of race and culture. Some theologians like Ada María Isasi-Díaz see the appropriation of mestizaje/mulatez positively, using it as locus theologicus for mujerista theology "precisely because it identifies our culture" and therefore "critiques the dominant culture against which we have to struggle to survive."[48]

While mestizaje and mulatez have opened us to take seriously the construction of race, these categories are inadequate in dealing with issues of globalization, pluralism, sexuality, and interreligious dialogue, to name but a few. Some, including Jean-Pierre

Ruiz and Néstor Medina, have addressed the limitations and sinful heritage of mestizaje and mulatez.[49] These critiques indicate that we cannot afford to forget, ignore, or conveniently and uncritically rehabilitate mestizaje and mulatez. This is particularly challenging for U.S. Hispanic theologians, for these categories have informed our theologizing for so long. With the recognition of our theologies, they have even acquired cross-over appeal.[50]

In our dependence on mestizaje we have too narrowly constructed hybridity discourse. While I remain conflicted over the ongoing value of using mestizaje/mulatez, I do appreciate the possibilities it has opened for dialogue. One of the challenges for Latin@ theologians is to seek out other expressions and constructions that also explore the complexities of hybrid identities.

For example, shifting the focus to linguistic diversity in the U.S. comunidad latina opens possibilities for deeper reflection on Spanglish as a locus theologicus. In the words of Ed Morales, our "Spanglish future" is "updated versions of liberation theology grafted onto post-Marxist prison gangs, like the Latin Kings, who hold meetings that are like a cross between a Catholic mass, a twelve-step meeting, and a slam poetry reading."[51] He continues, "To be Spanglish is to live in multisubjectivity; that is, in a space where race is indeterminate, and where class is slipperier than ever."[52] Theological reflection on language as an aspect of our hybridity allows for a long overdue conversation with popular culture and also offers another perspective for unpacking the multiple dimensions of our intraconnectedness.

## MULTIPLE BELONGING:
## DIVERSITY IN THE DIVINE IMAGE

Exploring identity in terms of an expanded understanding of hybridity as multiple belonging recognizes that human diversity is experienced as a belonging that is necessarily located, situated, embodied, engendered, and lived—culturally, linguistically, socially, economically, politically, racially, religiously, sexually, spiritually. This hybridity is grounded in a shared humanity and derived from creation in the divine image, which imparts a foundational commonality that must dictate the minimum level of expectation in our ethical behavior toward each other on the micro and macro levels.

Our embodied particularity is experienced as multiple belonging through a variety of biological, geographical, and relational factors. What we seek is not sameness but points of intersection that allow us to engage. According to Hawaiian author Darrell Lum, the impulse to establish relationality in this context is critical to understanding local culture which is also polycultural. For example, in Hawaii, a typical conversation starter is the question, asked in Hawaiian Creole English (pidgin), "What school you went?" This question has "its root in the native Hawaiian way of identifying oneself by geography and genealogy."[53] Lum continues, "Rather than being a question that divides us, [it] is fundamentally an effort to discover how we are connected."[54] We do not need to become each other in order to be companions or kin; respect for diversity entails a search for intersections and connections. As such, this Hawaiian local ritual "is expressly a way for two people to begin discovering their relationships with each other, however distant, in order to talk stories that sprout on common ground. It is a way to begin weaving their histories together—and this defines friendship, or an aspect of it, local style."[55] This way of engaging with others across different contexts by privileging the local in a polycultural environment offers fruitful possibilities for further conversation with U.S. Hispanic theologians and our privileging of lo cotidiano, the daily, and our understanding of relationships through compadrazgo/comadrazgo.

At the same time, a critical appropriation of multiple belonging requires that attention be paid to the experience of multiple "not fitting in." Whether by choice or accident, as the result of others' cruelties or our own stances, this is also a reality that inclusion rhetoric glosses over. Explorations of our hybridity and multiple belonging must also include a sustained conversation regarding multiple not fitting in. Who gets left out in our constructions of identity and community? Who resides on our margins when we omit or ignore the stories of our intersections? Who is ostracized based on arbitrary criteria determining the norm? Who is privileged and who is excluded when a particular norm is assumed as common? Who is silenced? Who loses agency? Who are the gatekeepers controlling access?

As theologians arising from the heart of a people who constitute the plurality of the U.S. Catholic Church and the largest minority population in the United States, we need to understand ourselves in a new way—as a majority. Theologizing from this perspective of majority, our past and contemporary experiences of marginalization have sensitized us to the dangers of privileging certain particularities and of inflating their significance with universal import. La comunidad latina is not the church's diversity. We *are* the church! Our contextual horizons charge us as theologians to question and critique current operative paradigms that fail to recognize diversity as constitutive of our human, national, and ecclesial conditions. Our contextual horizons invite us as theologians to pursue new directions for further exploration of diversity as these have ethical, practical, and pastoral implications.

# 2

## Decolonizing Practical and Pastoral Theologies

There are as many definitions of pastoral theology and practical theology as there are theologians, let alone denominational and congregational understandings. While some use these terms interchangeably and others perceive significant distinctions, in one area they share a vacuum: Latin@ theologians are virtually absent, as partners and resources, in shaping agendas, strategies, and discourse in the scholarship of both pastoral and practical theologies. Our presence in published works is treated as relatively new and/or emerging, with but a passing reference to a growing yet rarely cited body of literature.[1] Self-defined spiritualogian (theologian of spirituality) Gilberto Cavazos-González has described this as a racism of omission.

A number of possible reasons explain this absence. Some authors who write in the field of practical theologies hold a misconception that Hispanic theologies are indistinguishable from their Latin American counterparts and do not comprise a separate body of reflections arising from U.S. contexts. They assume that their inclusion of the scholarship of prominent liberation theologians like Gustavo Gutiérrez suffices as an articulation of experiences of theological latinidad.

On the other hand, some Latin@s do not identify exclusively as pastoral or practical theologians except with reluctant accommodation to the categories of the academy.[2] To claim identity as either a practical or a pastoral theologian often conveys a degree

21

of academic second-class citizenship. For Latin@s, whose theologies already experience marginalization, this is not an advantage, especially when others seek to classify our theologies as practical as a means of dismissing the value these scholarly contributions offer the wider church and academy.

The primarily European and Anglo–North American roots of the discipline and its methods serve also to limit its appeal for Latin@s. The concept that pastoral or practical functions as an adjective to describe theologizing is counterintuitive to a methodological approach distinctive to doing theology latinamente, an approach that appreciates theologizing as a process of mutual accountability, as teología y pastoral de conjunto. In the words of Jean-Pierre Ruiz:

> Theological analysis cannot be divorced either from the grassroots realities of religious experience or from conscientious involvement in pastoral practice. This necessary reciprocal connection keeps the U.S. Hispanic/Latino theology from becoming a self-enclosed, self-preoccupied endeavor by binding both its questions and its reflections to the lived reality and the living faith of the churches and communities within which and for the sake of which it takes place.[3]

From such a perspective, theology is necessarily public both in its method and in its sources, as the locus theologicus, the place of theologizing, is lo cotidiano, daily lived experience. The daily is not monolithic as the diversity of theological reflection emanating from Hispanic theologians demonstrates. Grounded in experiences of vida cotidiana (daily living), theologians vary regarding the particular lenses that inform their respective theologizing from their daily places. Attention to the daily focuses through specific lenses that include but are not limited to hybridity/mestizaje/mulatez; diasporas/migrations; las luchas/struggles endemic to poverty, oppression, injustice, colonization; experiences of women; spirituality and liturgy; popular religion and popular culture. These hermeneutical preferences reflect the daily living of the communities which individual theologians accompany and/or from which they arise as well as their own social location. In the words of Fernando Segovia, "At a fundamental level I have used my life story as a foundation for my work as a critic in biblical studies, as a theologian in theological studies, and as a critic in cultural studies. . . . I have relied on both the individual and the social dimensions not as binary oppositions but as interrelated and interdependent."[4]

Like Segovia and my other Latin@ colleagues, my own social location influences the lenses I use to interpret daily lived experience. Migration is one of the lenses through which I read lo cotidiano. Soy nieta de inmigrantes. My parents are bilingual children, among the first generation in their respective families, born as U.S. citizens. On the family tree for La Familia Fernández, painstakingly prepared by mi tía Connie, I find mi abuelo Emilio amid the names of ten hijos y hijas de José Fernández y Carmen García. Four, including my grandfather, bear the marker "inmigró a los Estados Unidos." These simple words do not reveal the reasons for their journeys or explain away a curious notation regarding race for both mi abuelo y mi abuela. On the manifest of the ship that brings them to the U.S. from Spain, via a sojourn in Cuba, under "complexion" they are categorized as "dark."[5]

Migrations are not objects of disengaged study; they are sources of theological reflection that emerge from mi vida cotidiana, an intersection of past and present, of my own story and of commitments to the communities that inform my theologizing. Biblical scholar David Sánchez observes, "The process of relocating our interpretive points of departure . . . to our distinctive social locations is not simply an intellectual enterprise but is the primary impetus for the construction of discourses that initiate the process of liberation and decolonization."[6]

The reconceptualization of pastoral and practical theologies as public theology is a challenge to the privatization of religion, as Bonnie Miller-McLemore has observed, and this reconceptualization "attempts to analyze and influence the wider social order."[7]

Toward this end three areas of significance have emerged in recent scholarship that contribute to this shift from the personal to the public: a turn to experience; the influence of liberation theologies; and the construction of flexible, multidimensional identities.

## A TURN TOWARD EXPERIENCE

An appreciation of human experience as a grounding for theologies is now more prevalent across the theological spectrum and is articulated in ways that place experience in conversation with and/or correlation to scripture, the Christian tradition, and, in some cases, culture. These readings of the "signs of the times" draw from other disciplines, especially the social sciences, in order to understand, interpret, and unravel the complexities of human experience. However, implicit is a compartmentalization of human living, communicated through theological reflection methods that attempt to distinguish human living into distinct spheres. It is too easy to slip from distinction to separation and an uncritical acceptance of a demarcation between sacred and secular, public and domestic.

From the locus of daily lived experience these distinctions are not so obvious. How does one separate human experience from a Christian tradition that is inextricably tied to one's daily living? How can one distinguish culture as a distinct element in the expression of one's faith? Is there another place to live faith besides domestically and publicly? From Latin@ perspectives these distinctions make little sense. In part, this may be due to a presumed religious world view that has created what Eldin Villafañe calls *homo religiosus*, for whom "there is no area of life, no matter how trivial, that is not 'transmuted' by the religious sentiment. The depth of Hispanic religiosity cannot be fathomed by mere statistical qualification of church attendance . . . statistical surveys or religious profiles."[8] Quite simply, "the Hispanic American community is a theological community,"[9] a community where distinctions between sacred and secular are blurred or even non-existent.

## UNWRAPPING THE DAILY IN LATIN@ THEOLOGIES

One of the major contributions of Latin@ theologians to the "doing" of theology is the privileging of lo cotidiano, daily lived experience.[10] The significance of lo cotidiano and the need to reflect theologically on it were initially and primarily developed by Latinas. In the words of María Pilar Aquino:

> There may be other languages that reflect critically on our practices, but what makes Latina thought *theological* is that it formally focuses on our day-to-day practices sustained by the liberating visions and traditions of Christian religion and faith. . . . What makes Latina thought *liberative* is that it deliberately focuses on our daily activities aimed at transformation toward greater justice.[11]

Aquino challenges androcentric influences that ignore the effects of daily life on theological endeavors. Instead, she posits that theology done from Latin American feminist perspectives recognizes "that active paradigms, traditions, and categories supporting the social construction of reality reside and operate in the daily life of people. . . . In the daily life of people reside the values and categories on which social consensus is based."[12] At the same time, she maintains that lo cotidiano serves to critique dehumanizing and polarizing social systems, institutions, and relationships. "*Lo cotidiano* is understood as a *dynamis* that seeks to make hegemonic and universal the logic of human rights—including the rights to friendship, bread, employment and beauty."[13]

For Ada María Isasi-Díaz, lo cotidiano is descriptively, hermeneutically, and epistemologically significant as it pertains to Hispanic women, effectively granting such daily living its rightful place among what is considered important.[14] Descriptively, lo cotidiano entails such factors as race, class and gender, as well as relational interactions, faith expressions, and experiences of authority.[15] Hermeneutically, lo cotidiano serves as an interpretive lens through which the "stuff" of reality ("actions, discourse, norms, established social roles and our own selves"),[16] is perceived and evaluated. Epistemologically, lo cotidiano "is a way of referring to Latinas' efforts to understand and express how and why their lives are the way they are, how and why they function as they do."[17] The use of the daily as a theological source exposes knowledge in general and theological knowledge in particular as being fragmentary, biased, and provisional. For Isasi-Díaz, this affirms its use as an act of subversion.

For Orlando Espín, the foundational experience of daily life as it exists and is lived, is the "birthing place" of "an authentically U.S. theology of grace from a Latino/a perspective."[18] Espín is careful not to reduce lo cotidiano to living that occurs primarily within the private or domestic sphere, and he acknowledges the impact on daily life of such macro factors as violence, poverty, global economics, information technology, politics, education, and media.

The focus on lo cotidiano has tended to favor a more positive or even hopeful interpretation of daily living, including that living which is marked by struggle and marginalization. Whether understood in terms of grace, salvific transformation, or la lucha, the discourse more often than not conveys an optimism that may unwittingly disguise a more sinful reality than we care to admit. Even Espín acknowledges, "If daily relations constitute the foundation and image for the totality of social relationships, then we must also arrive at the conclusion that the daily relationships of Latinos/as must be understood as experiences of sin."[19] Engaging in the messiness, the ambiguities, and the complexities of daily living empowers theologians and the communities they accompany to seek the transformation of injustice in the public arena as well as the domestic, in the rhythms and disruptions of ordinary living with "its routines and its surprises, its mysterious depths and its pedestrian quality."[20]

Domestic and foreign policies affect the daily living of actual, situated human beings: our kin, our neighbors, our parishioners, our colleagues and employees, our students, in other words, the communities we accompany as theologians. Risk clouds la vida cotidiana of those who dare to dream on the U.S. side of border fences. Benita Veliz, of San Antonio, Texas, is a St. Mary's University graduate who went from traffic court to possible deportation for an action beyond her control, her parents' journey across a border during her childhood. Though raised in the United States, her driving while alternately documented status became known when police stopped her for an alleged (minor) infraction. Benita's classmates held a rally at St. Mary's. Their bold act of solidarity sought to incarnate a statistic with the hopes that their action would encourage an act of Congress.

"What happens to a dream deferred?" the poet Langston Hughes once asked. Most of us are familiar with the response to this rhetorical question: "Does it dry up like a raisin in the sun?" Fewer of us know the rest of the poem, where the condition escalates to the point that the poem concludes, "Or does it explode?"[21] In the United States we have currently created the conditions for a permanent invisible but in-plain-sight underclass of young people with little hope. Optimistic about the so-called American dream, they learn, after they have followed what they thought were the rules, that their true identity precludes them from further dreaming. These alternately documented—by now Spanglish-speaking—kids discover, usually in their teens, that they cannot move on because, unlike their younger brothers or sisters, they were not born legally in the United States. With limited options and the fear of returning to las tierras they do not know, these kids live and work in the shadows.

On Easter Sunday 2009 ACHTUS reaffirmed its ongoing commitment to immigration reform with the release of a statement by its board urging, with the bishops of the United States, passage of the DREAM Act (Development, Relief, and Education for Alien Minors Act).[22] With this statement, consistent with its 2006 "Statement on Just, Comprehenive and Humane Immigration

Reform," ACHTUS exercised its public voice as scholars. The 2006 statement makes clear that it is precisely "through our scholarship and our ministries" that the academy will "commit ourselves to dispel falsehoods about immigration, to protect civil rights, to promote justice, and to make known the gifts, talents, and contributions of immigrants to our society."[23] The DREAM Act statement explicitly ties this particular commitment to concrete daily lived experiences of the corporate body as "an association of scholars, whose members are primarily teachers, researchers, administrators and graduate students in colleges, universities and seminaries across the United States and Puerto Rico"[24]

The timing of ACHTUS's DREAM Act statement was not accidental. On April 3, 2009, Bishop John C. Wester, chair of the USCCB Committee on Migration, on behalf of the conference, sent letters expressing support of the Act to Senator Richard Durbin (D-IL) and Senator Richard Lugar (R-IN), primary sponsors in the U.S. Senate, and Representative Howard Berman (D-CA) and Representative Lincoln Díaz-Balart (R-FL), primary sponsors in the U.S. House of Representatives.[25] Sadly, this received little if any mainstream media attention, even in the Catholic press; however, it found some life online in the blogosphere, on social networking sites, and on activist websites. The significance of such support by a faith community with one of the largest educational systems in the world was missed. Instead, the educational issue of the day was the Catholic identity of the University of Notre Dame with regards to the commencement appearance of President Barack Obama.[26]

## THEOLOGIES AS LIBERATING PRAXIS

Pastoral theologian Bonnie Miller McLemore maintains that the effects of liberation theology were such that "few, if any, contemporary pastoral theologians or counselors have escaped its impact."[27] Miller McLemore contends that liberation theology "helped transform pastoral theology toward public theology by identifying the ways in which society indelibly constructs selfhood in oppressive ways, by redefining the nature of the public, and by demanding a prophetic reorientation towards it."[28]

The appropriation of liberation theologies beyond their original contexts in Latin America and in U.S. African American communities of the 1970s and 1980s, however, failed in many cases to take into account the particularity of these theological expressions. On the other hand, influenced by Latin American liberation theologies, Hispanic theologies arose approximately thirty years ago out of a U.S. context, addressing particularly U.S. experiences of oppression. For example, Latin@ theologians like Virgilio Elizondo responded to oppression experienced through cultural markers (such as discrimination based on language, color, ethnicity, condition of hybridity) that in effect resulted in economic, political, and even religious marginalization of particular communities. Elizondo theologizes from daily lived experiences of Mexican Americans in the southwestern United States, a people who, though treated as aliens, historically had not crossed the border but whose Mexican ancestors had been crossed by the expansionist practicalities of manifest destiny in the 1840s. For Elizondo, reconceptualizing hybridity as a new creation reveals the salvific significance of mestizos/as for all humanity. He took that which was despised and a cause for self-deprecation, and through restorative liberatory praxis reenvisioned hybridity as revelatory of the Divine.

Cuban Americans like Orlando Espín and Roberto Goizueta challenged Latin American liberationists' dismissal of popular religion and the U.S. reduction of popular religious expression to quaint folk status. Their work uncovers the religion of the people as liberatory praxis. In U.S. contexts Latin@ liberating theologies necessarily theologized through lenses that bore cultural significance precisely because these markers were inseparable from economic, social, political, and religious marginalization. Sadly, not much has changed. Heed the words of former Colorado governor Richard Lamm, from his 2006 book *Two Wands, One Nation*:

I suggest that groups whose culture and values stress de-
layed gratification—along with education, hard work, success and ambition—are those groups that succeed in
America, regardless of discrimination. I further suggest that,
even if discrimination were removed, that other groups
would still have massive problems until they developed the
traits that lead to success. Asian and Jewish children do
twice as much homework as black and Hispanic students,
and get far better grades. Why should we be surprised?[29]

The U.S. context is further complicated by the comparatively
more promising access to economic stability. To acknowledge
this reality is neither to disregard the disenfranchisement of this
nation's poorest people nor to ignore the disproportionate gap
in wealth between our poorest and richest citizens and residents.
Instead, to do so is to acknowledge the presence and lure of the
vast economic middle. While the poverty rate in the Latin@ population, at 21.8 percent, is almost three times that of whites,[30]
this same community boasts a coveted consumer power. Latin@s
constitute the fastest-growing consumer market, with a purchasing power that approached US$1 trillion in 2009.[31]
    Ethnographic research of the Mexican and Puerto Rican com-
munities in Chicago points to the challenges associated with educational and economic attainment in relation to the construction of latinidad and socioeconomic class.[32] Interviews by
Nicholas de Genova and Ana Ramos-Zayas indicated that self-
identification as Latino/a and/or Hispano/a, by upwardly mo-
bile and aspiring middle-class Puerto Ricans and Mexican Americans, especially the college educated, intentionally distanced
individuals from particular communal identifications that marked
them as either alien (for Mexicans) or under class (for Puerto
Ricans). These umbrella identifications "presented an alterna-
tive to the most stigmatized aspects of 'Mexican' or 'Puerto Rican'
identity by affirming substantive affiliations with less stigmatized groups of Latin American descent."[33] In effect, the "process of becoming 'middle-class' was consonant with 'becoming

Latino.'"[34] This confirms a caution raised by author Juan Flores in *From Bomba to Hip Hop*, namely, that "generic, unqualified usage" of these terms can at times be employed to

> mislead the public into thinking that all members and con-
> stituents of the composite are in basically the same posi-
> tion in society and all are progressing toward acceptance
> and self-advancement from the same starting line, and at
> the same pace . . . Thus what presents itself as a category
> of inclusion and compatibility functions as a tool of exclu-
> sion and internal "othering."[35]

At the same time, interviews suggested that upward mobility did not necessarily preclude "an acute sense of their own consequent responsibilities, as indicated by a persistent emphasis on 'giving back' to their communities."[36]

One oversight of theologies of liberation is a failure to name the goals of liberating praxis according to their particular contexts. This results in an inability to identify liberation concretely in terms of "from what and/or toward what." Abstractions like human fulfillment are insufficient in response to the allure of the gospel of prosperity. The Pew Hispanic Center's 2007 study "Changing Faiths" reaches a disturbing conclusion that requires deeper analysis and explication. "Regardless of religious tradition, Latinos also largely subscribe to views sometimes described as the prosperity gospel, the belief that God rewards the faithful with physical well-being and financial prosperity in this life. About three-in-four Latino Catholics, evangelicals and mainline Protestants subscribe to this view."[37]

If liberation is more than just an eschatological hope, then its realization, even partial, needs to be addressed. In other words, "now what?" What happens when some measure of well-being is achieved? When struggle bears fruit? When some of the disenfranchised are politically and economically enfranchised? When surviving becomes thriving? When the marginalized move toward the mainstream, or at least their children do? This phenomenon has already been observed in the pervasiveness of Latin@ popular culture:

> While for many, everyday survival in the geocultural borderlands . . . continues to be an existence of pain and powerlessness, many Latino/a cultural productions are becoming incorporated into the U.S. mainstream . . . made possible in part by access to education and power gained as a result of the Civil Rights movement. [This mainstreaming] also serves as a gatekeeping mechanism by which the dominant sector mediates and contains the political power of these self-representations.[38]

In the shift from the underside to the mainstream how do communities avoid cooptation and complicity in their own neocolonization? How do constructive theologies account for the complex factors that create transformation? For example, some Latin@ scholars and activists note the profound influence of military and civilian service during World War II in securing civil rights for Hispanics, especially in the case of Mexican Americans. The role of returning veterans, disgruntled by their treatment at home after proving their loyalty to their nation, adds a problematic level to idealistic transformation narratives as does the economic advancement achieved by civilian workers in war-related industries.

> The war promised great things to Mexican Americans, and delivered in a number of areas. They gained greater access to better jobs, their civil rights demands for the first time were being addressed (albeit inadequately), and their status as full contributing members of the American community was recognized. None of this was likely to have happened when it did without the pressures of war.[39]

It is too easy to dismiss the sinful dimension that may accompany transformation. While it is not the intention here to question the legitimacy of U.S. involvement in World War II, it would be irresponsible to ignore the intricacies and moral ambiguities that can be tightly interwoven into the fabric of justice.

From liberative perspectives in U.S. contexts, pursuit of the American dream—employment, economic security, educational attainment, security in old age, health care, and the possibility of home ownership—for oneself and, more important, for one's children, is a powerful motivator. How is solidarity nurtured in contexts of realized liberation, no matter how partial? How does our theologizing cultivate daily, just, and relational concern for those who struggle, when in reality basic human rights are barely secured in a working middle class that is facing a precarious future with its threats of un/underemployment, foreclosure, and even bankruptcy? Engaging the middle class or the rising middle class is not a priority for most liberation theologizing. In making preferential options for the poor, the not-so-poor forget that poverty, no matter how spiritualized, is not a desired permanent condition, though it may be a generational cyclic reality. The stereotyping of Hispanic communities as poor dismisses our own complex constructions of class and the transnational dimension of Latin@ economic clout. It is worth remembering that the salaries of restaurant, maintenance, agricultural, and hotel workers support whole villages back home, and many a nanny, construction worker and dish washer saves to build a retirement home por alla, wherever "over there" might be.

Among his critiques of European theologies, R. S. Sugirtharajah determines, "The object of English theology is the person who has come of age, whereas that in the case of liberation theology, as Gutiérrez has been repeatedly reminding us, is the person who has yet to become a person."[40] Sugirtharajah contrasts the "secular person who has come of age fed on Enlightenment values such as reason and human progress"[41] with liberation theologies' interlocutor, "the 'nonperson,' the human being who is not considered human by the present order—the exploited classes, marginalized ethnic groups, and despised cultures."[42] Who are the interlocutors for Latin@ theologians in the U.S.

context? The object and subject are a multilingual, polychromatic, transnational, intergenerational, pluricultural, panethnic gente whose experiences vary by geography, documented status, educational achievement and socioeconomic aspiration.

## LA VIDA BEYOND THE HYPHEN

In an age when migrations shape and reshape national imaginaries and geographies, theological reflection cannot afford to gloss over complex constructions of identity. In la comunidad latina the prevailing metaphor to make sense of the dynamic relationship between difference and unity has been the "hyphen." The concept of "life on the hyphen" evolved in literature, culture studies, and theology to describe a daily reality experienced by Latin@s, those of us who are immigrants as well as those of us with well-established roots in what is considered the United States. From the perspective of biblical scholar Fernando Segovia, a hyphenated identity brings a certain set of advantages. Straddling two worlds, one seeped in Iberian and Latin American-influenced cultures and the other more conversant with U.S. expectations, life on the hyphen makes one fluent in both worlds and allows one to function simultaneously as insider and outsider. In Segovia's words, "We can see what is good and bad in each world and choose accordingly; and we are able to offer an informed critique of each world—its vision, its values, its traditions."[43] Chronicling the Cuban American experience, Gustavo Pérez Firmat concludes, "In our case, the hyphen is not a minus sign but a plus, perhaps we should call ourselves 'Cubans plus Americans.'"[44]

From this paradigm arose educational, pastoral and political responses that have sought and continue to seek means of preserving bicultural and bilingual inheritances. However, what inevitably has resulted is a separate but not equal model, whereby other cultures and languages are perceived as optional upgrades or add-ons for those who understand themselves as Americans in a U.S.-Anglo land and/or accommodations for those outsiders who really do need to assimilate into the multicultural national and even ecclesial salad.

For example, in the traditioning of our faith, our popular devotions, our vernaculars, our ways of relating, our theologies are nice for nuestra gente, but this is a particularity that does not necessarily inform how the church universal prays together, functions together, let alone relates en conjunto. Only those who live on the hyphen are required to be bilingually fluent and biculturally aware. This hyphenated existence carries disadvantages. To borrow from Segovia again, "We are a people who live in two worlds and find ourselves at home in neither."[45]

There is much to learn from our young, from Generations Ñ and beyond. Identity in the twenty-first century is more complicated than hyphenated existence suggests. I would propose that identity today is experienced less as a matter of life on the hyphen and more as life on the "at" sign, el arroba, or, as I prefer to call it in mi Espanglish, el @. The incarnation of hybridity today collapses simple binary constructions and introduces new ways to conceptualize identity within a necessary convivencia that, it could be argued, is one of the goals of public policy.

What does identity reconfigured on @ signify, and what are its implications for convivencia? First of all, the @ signifies that there is connectedness, an intersection of interests, needs, or purpose that is also situated, located "at" a particular somewhere that shapes the perspectives of the name that precedes el arroba in an email address.

Second, @ signifies a "situatedness in motion."[46] For those of us raised in cyber culture, boundaries are porous. Cyberspace provides opportunities for intercultural exchanges in a nanosecond. *Text* is now a verb, no longer a static noun that must be probed and prodded to reveal its secrets. *Text* indicates the medium, action, and speed with which one can respond or mobilize response. To a degree, digital technologies and networking applications level the proverbial playing field, creating spaces for those traditionally excluded from public conversations. The grassroots cyber sophistication of Barack Obama's presidential campaign is but one example of the power of the Internet. This medium with its multiple possibilities for strategic engagement is also highly favored by those seeking immigration reforms through the DREAM Act, a movement that online is primarily student driven.

With unprecedented access comes a plethora of voices, but not always civility. Life on el @ does not automatically result in convivencia, but in the cyber plaza public theologizing cannot afford to be absent.

Third, life poised at @ signifies a flexibility that allows individuals and communities to hold multiple identities in creative tension. Life on @ in some ways resembles what journalist Ed Morales has coined our "Spanglish future," in other words, life lived with its multiple belongings that blur the lines of race, class, nation, and in some ways even gender.[47] This reality, with all its polychromatic, multilingual, intercultural, and transnational dimensions, invites skilled negotiations if there is to be hope for convivencia.

In this fluid context of multiple, intersecting connections, methods dependent on the Belgian Catholic Action axiom—"see, judge, act"—are necessarily subject to critique. Implicit in the terms of seeing, judging, and acting is a degree of distance and an assumption that there is much time for this process to unwind. One can get the sense of being an objective observer. The risk is that observers too often are disconnected, and it is that lack of being implicated that can and has caused a colonizing, disempowering, and denigrating loss of agency, especially for minoritized communities. Sometimes this occurs with the best of intentions, as the conscientized "haves" ignore the complex power differentials that truly shape our local and global relationships.

To learn to read context as a "text of our daily living" involves an admission that when we read we are always situated; there are no neutral readings. The reader located before el arroba is, in the words of Segovia, a "flesh and blood reader, historically and culturally conditioned, with a field of vision fundamentally informed and circumscribed by such a social location."[48] Reading involves interpretation, and reading and interpretation are in and of themselves praxis. Reading our texts and contexts is best accomplished within communities of interpreters. It is in the tension and humor, the agreements and the disagreements, that we are challenged to perceive the particular before us and respond anew from multiple perspectives.

For our Web 2.0 Generation Ñ, "see, judge, act" is an ancient linear paradigm that moves far too slowly in a cyber age where communication occurs in a keystroke. We are now taught to think in terms of networks of relationships; traditioning occurs through hypertexts, in other words, through multiple connections. The boundaries between participant and observer quickly become blurred in a world where blogging and instant messaging make engagement possible worlds apart but in real time.

Even in cyberspace, the word incarnate invites full and active participation. For theologies that privilege practice, the ultimate goal is not conversation but a just living together that is negotiated and renegotiated. To borrow from Gary Riebe-Estrella, the "vida found in lo cotidiano . . . is understood within our sociocentric cultural world as a shared reality . . . not simply vivencia, but convivencia."[49] By focusing on convivencia, literally our cohabitation, Latin@ theologies reflect on "the intimacy out of which la vida comes" and within which our theologies are embedded. From this stance, with all its tensions and hopes, it becomes possible to accompany faithfully our communities of accountability, in a manner cognizant of the "dynamic relationship of our particularity to other particularities."[50]

# 3

# Ortho-proxy and Orthopraxis

## The Ethics
## of Right Representation

In his 1993 debut album appropriately entitled *Represent*, gangsta rapper Fat Joe, aka Joseph Cartagena, establishes his "street creds" with vulgarities. Fat Joe locates himself through his rhyme relationally and geographically: "My name is Fat Joe I got [*expletive deleted*] locked down, Runnin' with the Latins and the blacks from Uptown," and then a few lines later he identifies his social location as a Puerto Rican coming from the Bronx.[1] With a vocabulary shot through with violence, he confirms his rapping skills and his ability to speak with an authority grounded in experience. The implication is that Joe can represent because he is situated in the reality of which he raps. The way he uses the language of the streets and their harsh reality as metaphor for his adversarial relationship with competing and established rappers underscores his claim.

As an Hispan@ born and raised in the Bronx, my identity is as tied to that tierra as Joe's, yet our experiences vary. At the same time, as a theologian I understand his need to establish street cred. Credibility is imperative when speaking in place of others, though I remain concerned about the ease with which one can move from representation to stolen agency.

## RIGHTLY AND RESPONSIBLY REPRESENTING OTHERS

When I accepted an invitation to speak in Minnesota, I ventured with humility and apprehension to expound on matters Latin@ as they applied to youth and—inevitably—to immigration. I spoke of daily living and its destructive disruptions as experienced by our alternately documented hermanas y hermanos. While I am the grandchild of immigrants, and my own vida cotidiana provides me with both context and commitment, I remain cautious about the credibility I have when speaking in the place of or about others. At a break in the program, a young Latina approached me for conversation. She expressed support and urged me on, saying, "I just want to jump up and say to the group, Listen to her! She's right!" Flattered, I responded naively that she should indeed feel free to speak out in the session. She replied, "I can't," for she was one of the alternately documented, and so her speaking out might draw the sort of unwanted attention that could devastate her family. Even in an apparently safe context, she could not take the chance. In this particular case the responsibility of representing entailed guaranteeing agency for another, by speaking as proxy for one whose security and livelihood would be compromised if she dared risk speaking herself.

Too often there is a temptation—even with the best of intentions—to move from solidarity with an other to a misguided assumption of commonality such that the other's agency is usurped. In other words, my good intentions, our shared humanity, and my particular experiences of you and with you can lead me to believe that I can represent you and in turn speak for you and in your place. The result is a denial of agency for those who are being represented, reinforcing their under-representation. The challenge is whether it is possible to exercise a posture of what I would call *ortho-proxy,* a term coined here to express the posture of rightly and responsibly representing another, in other words, ortho-proxy. For Latin@ theologians, our claims for engagement with our grassroots communities en conjunto place this concern close to the center of our commitments. For Latin@s, even in the church and academy, loss of agency is not an alien experience, because others (from mostly non-Hispanic communities) decide to translate, interpret, represent, or introduce us and our works, our ideas, needs, and customs to the broader community. We are left under-represented even in initiatives designed by others allegedly to ensure our enfranchisement. Treated as tokens, we are visible but are assumed to be incapable of analyzing our own needs and articulating the strategies to address them.

Access means agency, and so solidarity should never imply a loss of agency. The process of accompaniment employs a metaphor of walking with another, not stealing his or her shoes. The relationship between agency and representation is an ethical one. Ecclesiologies that claim to make preferential options for those among us who are vulnerable and/or on the margins will remain inadequate as long as language and practice employ distinctions between the first person "we," who are church, making an option for the third person "them," who are poor, immigrant, stranger, or any other classification of otherness that diminishes agency.

## MISREPRESENTATION: AN EPISCOPAL EXAMPLE

Revisiting the restructuring of the USCCB first discussed in Chapter 1 may prove instructive on matters of representation as well as on our earlier discussion of diversity. In November 2006 the U.S. bishops voted to approve the restructure proposal. This massive overhaul would cut diocesan assessments to the conference by 16 percent, reduce the number of standing committees from thirty-six to sixteen, and downsize the national staff by 125 positions.[2] Key to the reorganization was the establishment of five priority goals for the 2008–11 planning cycle. After some debate about its wording, the fifth goal emerged as "Recognition of cultural diversity with special emphasis on Hispanic ministry 'in the spirit of Encuentro.'"[3] The added emphasis on Hispanic ministry came at the insistence of several bishops, "led by Archbishop José H. Gómez of San Antonio, who objected that 'cultural diversity' alone did not capture the bishops' intense concern."[4]

At one level this inclusion seems a monumental step forward for Hispanic ministries, recognition of the significance of la comunidad latina for the church. However, among the victims of the reorganization was the Committee on Hispanic Affairs and the Secretariat for Hispanic Affairs and among the retirements effective July 1, 2007, was Ronaldo Cruz, executive director of the secretariat. In his 2006 Christmas/New Year's message, Cruz explained that "the offices for African and African American Catholics, Asian/Pacific Islanders Catholics, Hispanic/Latino Catholics, and Native American Catholics and Pastoral Care of Catholic Immigrants, Refugees and Travelers become one team working collaboratively" under the umbrella of a new Committee on Cultural Diversity in the Church.[5]

The reorganization effectively dismissed the concerns raised in 2001 by a group of regional and national leaders in Hispanic ministry. These leaders expressed reservations about "multicultural" models that would consolidate minorities under one umbrella, thus diluting the particular identities and visions of the absorbed ethnic ministries. Besides concerns over access to limited resources, they recognized the potential of such an arrangement to further distance Hispanic ministry staffs from their respective bishops, thereby excluding Latin@s from pertinent decision-making processes in their own church. They wondered about the overall effect on the church's ministries and mission.[6]

In practice, this reorganization placed over half of the U.S. Catholic Church under the aegis of one office in the bishops' conference, without apparent plans to increase its staffing significantly. The impact of this decision will probably be felt hardest at the local and diocesan levels. It is extremely shortsighted for the immediate future, when one considers that over "50% of

all Catholics in the United States under age 25 are of Hispanic/
Latino(a) descent."[7]

The restructuring serves effectively to homogenize difference
and squelch agency. What message about church is sent by the
creation of an umbrella committee that arbitrarily ascribes diversity as a characteristic of select communities? Is our episcopal leadership unintentionally complicit in the whitewashing of
countless generations of immigrants? If one does not fall under
the aegis of the Cultural Diversity Committee, then what does
that make one? For, in the words of David Roediger, "Whiteness
describes not a culture but precisely . . . the empty and therefore
terrifying attempt to build an identity based on what one isn't
and on whom one can hold back."[8]

Shifting demographics invite a deeper response than cosmetic-
surgery and greeting-card ecclesiologies. Pastoral praxis, theological reflection and analysis cannot be disconnected from the
greater discourse on identity, difference, belonging, hybridity,
and diversity taking place in the academy and in popular culture. Theological exploration of the misunderstanding of diversity that underlies these pastoral changes generated at the episcopal level and lived at the parish level invites deconstruction
and an ethical re-imagining. Ecclesiological visions that ignore,
obfuscate, and minimize the contextuality of our individual and
communal lives ultimately lead to an erasing of identities that
those of us in marginalized and minoritized communities have
struggled to articulate and get taken seriously in the church, academy, and society. Biblical scholar R. S. Sugirtharajah's observations about a current climate "suspicious of representation,
agency, and self-identity" are worth considering as the USCCB's
priorities favor an uncritical embrace of multicultural paradigms
with strategies that seek to level a playing field that is suddenly
perceived as being uneven when the present and future of the
church is praying in Spanglish. Sugirtharajah writes:

> Why is it that, at a time when previously silenced people have
> begun to script their own stories and speak for themselves,

the West celebrates the death of the author and proclaims
that the megastories are over. The West is currently experiencing the loss of grand discourse and is frowning at the
idea of the power of agency, at a time when the subalterns
are trying to make their stories heard.[9]

Representation based on undifferentiated sameness or uncritical accompaniment results in this case in a profound loss of
agency for those communities already under-represented in the
leadership of the church and in ministry on all levels. This mis-
representation has praxeological consequences, especially within
communities served primarily by those who come from outside
those communities and those whose pastoral formation and theological education lack substantive engagement with the scholarship arising from within the hearts of these communities. Who
determines what is best, for whom, and on what basis? For example, the nagging refrain from too many Anglos working in
Hispanic communities about the need for evangelization and
catechesis can just as easily betray an ignorance of or even bias
against the role of popular religious practice in traditioning the
faith.

## ETHICAL DIRECTIONS

Openness to our own lived experiences and claiming our own
voices should open us to recognize the value of the stories, voices,
and daily lived experiences of others. The privileging of lo
cotidiano in Latin@ theologies is mirrored in challenges articulated by scholars from other marginalized communities. Gay U.S.
philosopher Sean O'Connell reminds us that truly liberative
praxis

cannot operate within the limits of promoting some normative ideal, or even of evaluating possible candidates for
social action, such as the realization of social justice. Rather,

it must expand its parameters to engage critically the stories informing people's lives, stories that likewise inform the social ideals pursued. For such critical engagement to occur, it must promote strategies that encourage vulnerability to the stories of others, for one cannot engage critically what one does not take seriously.[10]

Doing theology responsibly calls for us to appreciate the fact that we do not toil alone. If we take seriously our engagement with the narratives and contexts of others' lived experiences, then we should be prepared to travel outside our own particular contexts and venture into possible zones of discomfort.

The realization that all theologies are local and contextual and that the macro and micro, global and local, globalizing and daily lived are inextricably connected serves as correctives for tendencies that universalize the particular or that demonize and/or romanticize either side of these equations. Contextual theologies, like those that arise from the reflections of Latin@ theologians, unmask claims of those who confuse their particularity for the norm. However, as contextual theologians, we too must avoid succumbing to the same temptation we challenge. African American biblical scholar Brian Blount, at the conclusion of his book on New Testament ethics, honestly admits that the temptation to substitute in place of the dominant lens a different cultural lens, even a more liberating lens from a marginalized perspective, and to make it the source for drawing normative ethics, would merely perpetuate what he calls the "monologue" method. Blount writes:

> Though key players would have changed places . . . it would nonetheless have been ethics from a single lens masquerading as ethics for all. It may come to the point that liberation ethics does have such universal possibilities. But this is a conclusion that should be reached through conversation across cultural borders, not as has been historically the case, mandated as "ethical" from one culture to all others.[11]

Doing theology responsibly calls us to appreciate theology's "universalizing function," while recognizing the distinction between universalizing and totalizing. In the words of Robert Schreiter, this entails the ability of theology "to speak beyond its own context, and an openness to hear voices from beyond its own boundaries. Universalizing is not totalizing, which entails a suppression of difference and a claim to be the sole voice."[12]

With openness to hearing voices beyond the boundaries, Hispanic theologians (like other theologies committed to liberative praxis), have accepted our responsibility for bringing voices from the margins to the table. Our intentional situatedness within particular communities challenges Latin@ theologians to make space for those among us who have been silenced or whose perspectives have been denigrated or rendered impotent. Bringing perspectives to the table, ensuring access, is not the same as speaking for or in place of those who need to be heard and heeded, though ongoing vigilance is necessary to avoid transgressing the boundaries of right representation. For example, in his discussion of the role of male scholars with respect to their advocacy on behalf of their female colleagues, Jean-Pierre Ruiz notes:

> If our theologies are going to make a difference in redressing the multiple structural and institutional oppressions of women, then we must do more, lest we continue to be even unwittingly complicit through silence and neglect. At the same time, our advocacy must avoid the sort of patronizing behavior by which Latino male theologians claim to speak *for* Latinas in ways that keep them from speaking *for themselves*.[13]

This is an issue that even those who themselves belong to doubly marginalized communities grapple with on occasion. Ada María Isasi-Díaz writes: "I have always been concerned not only about speaking 'for' all Latinas but even as speaking 'for' any Latina. But the fact is that because *mujerista* theology is about creating a public voice, there is no other way to proceed but to speak whether 'as' or 'for.'"[14] O'Connell proposes another direction for liberative praxis:

> It must engage in enabling those who have no voice and who have no language that can do justice to the stories that they might tell to gain voice and to appropriate language, which in turn means enabling the speakers in society to hear the silence required for listening and to develop an attunement to the disruptive power of poetry at work in transformative stories.[15]

Even the creation of space for marginalized voices to speak or be heard is not unaccompanied by undertones of privilege. As Sharon Ringe observes, "Autonomy of agency or voice becomes even more complex. The very notion that we are in a position to 'let' other women speak for themselves maintains them in their role as 'subalterns.' Their speech is still instrumental to others' projects, even as that speech itself is channeled through the research and analyses of those others."[16]

Doing theology responsibly calls us to avoid further marginalization and to avoid unwittingly perpetuating the very cycles of injustice we claim to challenge as theologians who are engaged in struggles for liberation with communities who often are on the margins. This is especially challenging when those whose agency we work to promote are those who are dismissed as unsophisticated and underprepared to represent themselves. Creating public space for discourse, ensuring access, and—in limited circumstances—representing others who have entrusted us with that responsibility, call us to cultivate a habit of responsible listening. Dietrich Bonhoeffer once observed that ministers—and I would add theologians—"so often think they must always contribute something when they are in the company of others; they forget that listening can be a greater service than speaking."[17]

While much attention has been given to bringing the voices of marginalized individuals and communities to the table, less has been done to shift the burden of responsibility to those who must do the hearing and attending. If we are to be ethically responsible, then we must take care to listen so as not to misrepresent what is being said or to reinterpret it through the lenses of our own agendas. The example of some in the loosely constructed anti-globalization movement serves to illustrate the point. "While often their protests may be made on behalf of the poor, some of what they oppose is what the marginal and poor want to see happen—economic expansion, more and cheaper consumer goods, wider access to the middle class affluence which many Americans experience."[18]

## LECTORAS CAUSE TROUBLE

A provocative twist on representation can be found in biblical scholar Jean-Pierre Ruiz's retrieval of an obscure episode in U.S. Hispan@ and Cuban histories.[19] Ruiz recovers the story of los lectores (and occasionally las lectoras), the readers hired by cigar-factory workers, using their own wages, to read to them as they worked. Possibly arising from a practice in nineteenth-century Cuban jails, where lectors read aloud to inmates to help them while away the hours, cigar-factory workers adapted the practice to their own context, but it was the "workers, who democratically selected readings . . . including materials from the proletariat press and fiction with social themes."[20] Through this process, as Darien Cavanaugh explains, "a predominantly illiterate workforce became familiar with the writings of the great novelists and theorists of the time as well as working conditions in other parts of the world. . . . This informal working class education and the lectors' direct involvement with labor activity cut to the heart of the factory owners' distaste for the readers."[21] This was not a unilateral relationship, nor was power concentrated on the side of the more educated reader. The lectores received "the freedom to present radical ideas to a captive but willing audience."[22] The listeners, los oidores, simultaneously in their roles as both listener and employer, invested in their own education, and, according to Ruiz, "were empowered by what they learned, emboldened to become participants and not mere spectators."[23] This reality threatened the status quo and the power of the factory owners, and caused them to see the readers as "the ones who cause trouble." The empowerment and education of the oidores within their own daily context and by the fruits of their own labor reveal the complex relationship among representation, agency, and liberative praxis.

Ruiz also notes that a number of readers moved from performing the texts written by others to the creation of their own texts in a variety of media and genres. He draws particular attention to the enigmatic Puerto Rican lectora Luisa Capetillo, a heterosexual woman who dressed in the same formal clothes as her male counterparts, and whose gender was revealed to her listeners only when she opened her mouth. This "woman in men's clothing chosen by a mixed-sex work force to fill a traditionally masculine role"[24] further challenged male power by cross-dressing in her daily living as an act of emancipation, not collusion. Capetillo paid a price for her transgressive behavior, for she was arrested in Puerto Rico for cross-dressing, an act that disrupted the constructed order of gender conventions. She claimed agency by reappropriating that which would seek to deny it, and, like other lectores, she too moved from performing the texts of others to writing her own, maintaining integrity as a reader-writer-activist.

## ECCLESIOLOGY AND REPRESENTATION AS ACCOMPANIMENT

Ecclesiologies that arise from models of mutual accountability, from what we call in our Latin@ theologies the connection between teología y pastoral de conjunto, bear prophetic witness. Representation as ortho-proxy is found in the relationship between lectors and their communities of accountability and from the liberating orthopraxis that results from the communal engagement that nourishes and sustains all parties involved, yet challenges the status quo as well.

Current perceptions of Latin@ theologies within the academy and in too many of our churches sadly reflect the greater reality experienced by our communities daily. The words of performance artist and cultural theorist Guillermo Gómez-Peña about Latin@ art could just as easily apply to the reception of our theologies in the broader academy:

> We are undetermined "objects of desire." . . . The contemporary art [*theological*] world needs and desires the spiritual and aesthetic models of Latino culture without having to experience our political outrage and cultural contradictions. . . . Our art [*theology*] is described as "colorful," "passionate," "mysterious," "exuberant," "baroque," etc., all euphemistic terms for irrationalism and primitivism. [25]

As long as Hispanics remain the most under-represented community in theological education and pastoral ministry, we will have little impact on the agendas, strategies, discourses, and trajectories of our churches and of the academic venues that are of concern to us. If our concerns are being marginalized as exotic, it might even be better if they were ignored altogether. Our under-representation is underscored by the fact that "every area in the life of our institutions (curriculum, predominant pedagogies, personal and professional interaction) is reflective of a particular world view, which itself arises out of a particular context."[26] These contexts do not reflect our latinidad and, continuing in the words of Gary Riebe-Estrella, "we must challenge those pedagogies that have managed to insinuate themselves into the center of theological education and which are anchored in the power of those who are replicating their own training."[27] The genesis of Latin@ theologies is not the discovery and naming of the sinfulness of white privilege by those who are dominant in the academy.

The challenge of feminist biblical scholar Sharon Ringe serves as an appropriate caution for those seeking to re-image ecclesiology responsibly. Using the rubric of colonialism to understand the relationship of dominant culture women in the church and academy as both "victims and victimizers," Ringe reminds us such a "recognition overcomes the simple dichotomies of oppressor and oppressed, evil and wronged, 'bad' and 'good.'" She warns that the guilt such women carry for their reinforcement of that colonizing system "is not the guilt of overt malice (which we can quickly deny behind the defense of our 'liberal' or even 'radical' credentials), but rather the evil of collusion in a project that encompasses us and that, insofar as it benefits us, we find untroubling."[28]

Faced with our own under-representation, Latin@ theological scholarship takes on urgency and a responsibility to function as public and as resistant. The power to shape ecclesiologies also rests with those whom we accompany, those who populate our classrooms and our churches, nuestros barrios y nuestras familias, our transnational and particular communities of accountability.

# 4

# The *Imago Dei* in the Vernacular

Without a doubt, the concept of the *Imago Dei* plays a defining role in Latin@ theologies, an enterprise marked by particular development of theological anthropologies.[1] From the groundbreaking scholarship of Virgilio Elizondo in reenvisioning mestizaje as a legitimate reflection of the divine,[2] to Miguel Díaz's focus on the Trinity as ground for a relational theological anthropology,[3] the focus appears to remain for the most part on humanity. It is the question "Who are human persons?" that drives Orlando Espín to propose that it is time "to admit the complexity of our respective and shared identities and move beyond the insufficient, and ultimately sterile, descriptions of one another mostly in terms of only three contextualizations: race, culture, and gender."[4] In addition, it is this recognition of the *imago Dei* that fuels Ada María Isasi-Díaz's call for a lived praxis of justice necessary for building God's "kin-dom" in a manner worthy of our human kinship.[5] While at first glance these appear to be primarily contributions to theological anthropology, I would contend that for Latin@ theologians, human beings, in all our particularity, constitute revelatory texts. Our God-talk, in our vernacular, requires us to read in nuanced ways the contexts and contours of our situated humanity—in relationship. After all, theologies are the humble articulations of the perennially tongue-tied in the presence of mystery.

51

## A POSTCOLONIAL ESPANGLISH READ
## OF GENESIS 1:26–28

Then God said, "Let us make humankind in our image, according to our likeness; and let them have dominion over the fish of the sea, and over the birds of the air, and over the cattle, and over all the wild animals of the earth, and over every creeping thing that creeps upon the earth." So God created humankind in his image, in the image of God he created them; male and female he created them. God blessed them, and God said to them, "Be fruitful and multiply, and fill the earth and subdue it; and have dominion over the fish of the sea and over the birds of the air and over every living thing that moves upon the earth." (Gn 1:26–28, NRSV)

In many ways, thanks to my Latino colleagues in biblical studies (including Fernando Segovia, Jean-Pierre Ruiz, and Francisco Lozada), I am an accidental postcolonialist. I resonate with R. S. Sugirtharajah's understanding of postcolonialism as an enquiry, a catalyst, a way of life that "instigates and creates possibilities, and provides a platform for the widest possible convergence of critical forces, of multi-ethnic, multi-religious, and multicultural voices, to assert their denied rights and rattle the centre."[6] As one who relishes in rattling the center, I cannot help but read the Priestly tradition's account of human creation in the divine image (Gn 1:26–28; 5:1–2; 9:6–7) as a political theology of representation. *Ādām*, Hebrew for "human being," is created as male and as female.

This is a passage revisited with some frequency, especially by feminist biblical scholars and theologians, and its contested interpretations have too often ventured far into abstraction. Seminal to our focus is biblical scholarship that draws attention to the Priestly tradition's reliance on conventions of the day with respect to monarchs representing the deity. According to Helen

Schüngel-Straumann, "In Israel's environment, only outstanding persons qualify for that, whereas P regards all human beings as God's representatives. . . . The democraticization of an ancient oriental concept is particularly impressive in this case."[7]

The concept of representation in this passage implies power, agency, and difference. There is the power to rule, to have dominion, to administer in a way that is faithful to the one who is being represented. It is power with limitations, for as Schüngel-Straumann observes, "animals may not be killed and humans are not to rule over other humans: it is God's privilege to rule over humanity."[8] It is power that is exercised with responsible agency, whereby the blessed representatives participate both in the creating and in the caring.

There is the embrace of difference, *ādām*—as male and as female—is equally qualified to represent the Divine. This difference establishes otherness as constitutive of the Divine as well as of humanity. This is not about the gendering of God; rather, this passage locates diversity within the very being of God. In other words, God is like me and God is not like me, and God is like you, and not like you. Here too there has been a tendency to seek common ground as the basis of humanity's shared image, whereas the opposite is equally compelling: difference bears revelatory theological significance in the inexhaustible God. This is the conclusion of Fray Juan de Torquemada, a Franciscan missionary and historian, who tried to explain human difference and the racial variations among the peoples of his time. From his position in sixteenth-century Mexico he found that God must be the source of this "marvelous variety of colors," and so, diversity is an expression of divine intention, not an accident.

> There is no other reason for this than God's wish to display his marvels through the variety of colors. Like the colors of the flowers in a field, he wished for them to preserve that given to them by nature. In this way, just as God is praised in the many shades of flowers, so too is the Almighty blessed and praised in the different and varied colors of [*hu*]mankind.

It is through his artifices and paintings that he [God] chose
to show the boundlessness of his wisdom.[9]

Torquemada's theological reflection suggests that creation in
the divine image may actually say more about the richness of
God's diversity than it does about our own humanity. Retrieving
this insight from the depth and breadth of our Hispanic theological heritage provides direction for the development of new
paradigms that address la nueva realidad that is the Catholic
Church in the United States. Human creation in the divine image is creation in the divine diversity. Reflected in our embodied,
engendered, and located differences are the splendor, the complexity, and the very mystery of God.

## "EL OTHERCIDE, EL OTROCIDIO, DIGO, THE MURDERING OF OTHERNESS"[10]

Perhaps it comes as no surprise that a reminder of the divine
image returns in Genesis 5, positioned at the beginning of the
genealogy of the familia de *ādām* after the murder of Abel (Gn
5:1–2). It reappears a third time in Genesis 9, after the flood (Gn
9:6–7). One is left to wonder whether the Divine is reminding
humans of the responsibilities that the agency of representation
entails. Or is an exasperated God seeking to reassure the divine
self that this creation truly does bear the *imago Dei*? This passage takes on a poignant significance when placed in its immediate literary context. In the same chapter we find one of the most
destructive passages ever interpreted, Genesis 9:25–27, the curs-
ing of Ham/Canaan, a text that was used to justify the indefen-
sible—the African slave trade.

There is an unavoidable implication of our theologies in the
sins of exploitation, born of colonization and slavery. We are
compelled to address continuously a pivotal theological question that arises because of the Spanish colonial project in the
Americas: the question of the *imago Dei*. This is not only a mat-

ter of who is human, but it is also a matter of who can represent God, and in effect a matter of who God is said to be. Thus this is not solely an anthropological issue; it is profoundly theological.

These are also questions with practical implications lived out in the daily; theological understandings of the *imago Dei* affect everything from evangelization to intermarriage to migration. Para nosotros como Latin@s la teología concreta es sumamente importante. Lest we forget the ethical dimension inherent in nuestra teología y pastoral de conjunto, the words of seventeenth-century missionary and abolitionist Francisco José de Jaca de Aragón should haunt us to this day: "If the professors, theologians, confessors, religious men had not been silent dogs in the Indies, then iniquity and injustice would not have developed so enormously and without remedy."[11] Otrocide, the murder of otherness, the failure to comprehend the divine in the representative, the denial of agency, is a compound act of violence against God. It defiles the divine in both the self and in the other. In the words of Schüngel-Straumann, "Whoever attacks the image, attacks the prototype, God."[12]

## A HYBRID GOD IN MOTION

What does the image tell us about the prototype? In her exploration of latinidad, Juana María Rodríguez navigates intersections of lo popular and theory through a queer lens. She suggests that identity "is about situatedness in motion: embodiment and spatiality. It is about a self that is constituted through and against other selves in contexts that serve to establish the relationship between the self and the other."[13] Here is wisdom that finds resonance in certain expressions of Latin@ and Hispan@ popular Catholicism. Posadas, Pésames, Via Crucis, Camino de Santiago are for all practical purposes about embodiment and spatiality. They articulate, en la lengua cotidiana, an unabashedly incarnational perspective that grounds and guides our religious practices and theologies.

It is precisely this embodiment of loss, suffering, and longing that is re-created spatially in the here and now, in our contemporary and local geographies. It is no surprise, then, that the metaphor of accompaniment describes the unfathomable relationship between the human and the divine. As Raúl Gómez-Ruiz believes, these ritualized moments "represent the vulnerable, dependent Jesus who not only reflects human weakness and vulnerability but also requires human solidarity in suffering. This reveals to Hispanics that Jesus accompanies them in their lives and inspires them to accompany him in his suffering and death, his resurrection and exaltation."[14]

There is mutuality in this relationship, as Roberto Goizueta reminds us: the God who accompanies is in return accompanied, and this process of acompañamiento occurs in the very situated contexts of particular vidas cotidianas.[15] This is no mere re-creation, for in effect, as these rituals move through the familiar public square y los barrios, God accompanies and is accompanied—in the *imago Dei* of nuestros vecinos, our neighbors y de nuestr@s compañer@s—not in some abstract and rarefied way but in las luchas that are concrete and unsanitized:

- in the *imago Dei* of los vatos lost and those who mourn their untimely and unnecessary passing;
- in the *imago Dei* of the alternately documented parents in Chicago desperately trying to make sense out of the house fire that claimed the lives of their children;
- in the *imago Dei* of the dead and wounded returned home to a citizenship earned through service in war;
- in the *imago Dei* of the kids who go to school and try to do the right thing and of their classmates, whose fears drive them to commit the incomprehensible;
- in the *imago Dei* of the human beings rounded up like cattle by Immigration and Customs Enforcement agents, separated from their families, and warehoused with no access to legal representation;

- in the *imago Dei* of those for whom autism speaks, or for whom foreclosures loom, those with compromised health, or way too many bills too pay;
- in the *imago Dei* that defies simple categorization according to gender, race, ethnicity or culture.

Dios is in this motion of mutual acompañamiento, ritualized, lived, and reflected upon theologically. The observations of both Gómez Ruiz and Goizueta invite us to see these moments of ritualized struggle, in part, as resistance en conjunto, "as an active, communal undertaking" as opposed to "a suffering passively endured by a solitary individual."[16]

This is the passion and the life of the logos made flesh. What categories have we constructed as Latin@ that may shed light on the complexity of the embodied logos? Thomas Aquinas's daring cross-cultural explorations stretched the Christian imagination of his day by integrating the vocabulary of Aristotelian philosophy into Christian God-talk, a theological journey with roots in Muslim Spain. What about our talk about identity and hybridity? How do these categories generate new insights on the incarnation, or Trinity, insights accessible to more than just la comunidad latina?

How does hybridity (our concrete experiences of living hybridity) help us to re-imagine the identity of the word made flesh in terms that make sense for our times? Hybridity, as an intersection of difference, an embodiment of multiple belongings, is not a contradiction but a part of nuestras vidas cotidianas. I am *not* proposing mestizaje as a key to understanding the hypostatic union, nor am I canonizing a mestizo Galilean Jesus. These have served as first-line theological reflections that we have appropriately analyzed and critiqued. Naive appropriations, no matter how well intentioned, cannot rehabilitate categories with roots in violence and anti-Judaism. Yet these first-generation reflections cultivated the possibilities of re-imagining hybridity as a way to open up theological concepts like incarnation and

Trinity. From a postcolonial perspective, Joerg Rieger hints at some possibilities: "Jesus as fully divine and fully human 'hybrid' might pose the ultimate challenge to the empire's aspiration to clear-cut definitions and essences on which its power rests."[17]

We dare not deceive ourselves into thinking that God-talk of hybridity will be received warmly in the academy. Culture studies scholar William Anthony Nericcio reminds us that "half-breeds are both monsters and monstrous to the extent that they carry, hidden in their blood, illicit and untoward mixtures and speak to the corruption of the body and the most latent fears of the body politic."[18] Performance artist Guillermo Gómez-Peña reinforces this caution: "Artists who favor hybridity and cross-cultural collaboration are viewed with mistrust by all sides."[19]

In some ways it is not unusual that the question of the *imago Dei* is raised in the heart of the already multiply hybrid Spain at a time when this polychromatic, polyglot, interreligious context is simultaneously seeking to eradicate difference while exploring vistas that in effect increase its hybridity.[20] At the same time, it is not unusual that the question of the *imago Dei* is being raised in the heart of a hybrid United States by a polychromatic, polyglot, multiethnic, translocal comunidad of scholars seeking to articulate the multiple intersecting contexts that form the basis of fluid identities in relationship. Explorations into popular culture demonstrate that we are not the only scholars or artists for whom representation and hybridity are daily concerns. However, in our day theologizing en Espanglish also implies fluency in e-spanglish, as viral cyber-reality reshapes our notions of identity, community, and even ritual.

## EL PANADERO Y LA PLANCHA

In her book *Consider Jesus* Elizabeth Johnson records the development of conciliar Christology from the second through the seventh centuries. She observes that questions about the relationship between the divinity and humanity in Jesus "were phrased according to the idiom of the day, so that people of the church were involved in their development." Johnson continues: "Debate raged over Jesus Christ's identity. One bishop went out to buy a loaf of bread and wrote later that 'even the baker' wanted to discuss whether there were one or two natures in Christ!"[21] Peter Brown observes that these early doctrinal controversies ignited passions on the grassroots level so much so that "educated Christians spoke, though not always with enthusiasm, of the involvement of all classes in their quarrels."[22] He goes on to cite Gregory of Nyssa: "If you ask about your change, the shopkeeper talks theology to you on the Begotten and the Unbegotten; if you inquire about the price of a loaf, the reply is 'The Father is greater and the Son is inferior'; and if you say 'Is the bath ready?' the attendant affirms that the Son is of nothing."[23] Is this fourth-century public interest the equivalent of today's "Reality TV," offering a distraction amid economic insecurity? Whatever the reason, Rieger contends, "doctrines such as the matter of coequality were closely related to everyday concerns and real-life issues."[24] Theologizing in the vernacular is not new, and as the baker demonstrates, the concerns of theology are not abstract constructions but daily business.

Lo cotidiano is the locus of our theological reflection latinamente, and we vary the lenses that more sharply focus our attention. This privileging of the daily is enshrined in la plancha, the symbol of leadership for ACHTUS. Passed on from president to president, la plancha is a rusty nineteenth-century iron from Mexicali that is a work of art, not only because of the image painted on its base, but also in the daily art of the metalsmith whose hands shaped this implement for each day's labor. Nuestra plancha is about nuestro trabajo, and we can only hope for our theologies what poet and essayist Martín Espada hopes for the poems that are his craft:

I want to see poems pinned on the refrigerator, carried in wallets until they crumble, read aloud on the phone at

3 AM. I want to see poems that are political in the broad sense of urgent engagement with the human condition, poems that defend human dignity.[25]

Such are the words that honor the genius of nuestra plancha, an insistent instrument.

If we too are *imagines Dei*, then our God-talk in our vernacular is our unique contribution to theology. If our words get lost in translation, then maybe we should train a generation of translators—but we should not abandon the very insights upon which our theologies and our academy are founded.

Why do I care so much about what the baker thinks about theology? I care porque soy nieta de panadero. María Luisa, Anita, Carlitos (Chip), and I are the grandchildren of Emilio Fernández, the immigrant baker from Galicia, who lived for a short time in Havana, and who worked in New York. Sadly, he didn't live long enough to see his three niñas, my mother and her sisters, grow out of their childhood. However, there is no mistaking the gallego that lives on in two generations of his hybrid progeny, who make it our business to rattle the center on a daily basis.

# 5

## Handing on Faith
## en su propia lengua

In the February 2003 issue of *Vanity Fair* magazine satirical advice in a column by humorist Dame Edna struck a raw nerve. In a flippant response to a (fictitious) reader's question about the value of learning a foreign language, Dame Edna advised: "Forget Spanish. There's nothing in that language worth reading. . . . Who speaks it that you are really desperate to talk to? The help? Your leaf blower? Study German or French, where there are at least a few books worth reading, or, if you are American, try English."[1] If the cyber-storm that erupted in reply is any indication, the editors of *Vanity Fair* seriously underestimated the relationship between language and the construction and transmission of identity. The overwhelming response, which included boycotts and death threats, resulted in an explanation and an apology from the editors:

The backward bigotry of these statements was so far over the line that we felt it could only be taken as satire. In our judgment it was a politically incorrect but blatantly satirical barb directed against anyone who might be unaware of the great contributions Latin people have made and continue to make in every walk of life, here in the United States and around the world. (Note, too, that two sentences later,

61

she insults English-speaking Americans, saying, "If you're American, try [learning] English").[2]

Lost in the firestorm of opinions ranging from charges of racism to claims of Hispanic hypersensitivity was the sad reality that what seemed to author and editors blatantly satiric unfortunately reflected a slice of vida cotidiana in the United States. The fact that so many did not understand that this column was intended as a work of fiction, and that the writer's attitude was ironic, demonstrates that the bigotry portrayed in the column is still a part of the experience of too many U.S. Latin@s. Language is not neutral. "Language, after all, is at the heart of an individual's social identity. It is the vehicle through which the songs, folklore, and customs of any group are preserved and transmitted to its descendants."[3]

The significance of language in the navigation of boundaries and in the negotiation of identities within and across generations emerges as a legitimate and necessary locus for theological reflection. For faith communities in particular the role of language in the process of traditioning across generations has pastoral implications. If human identities are formed through "webs of interlocution"[4] then communities of discourse matter and the process of mutual engagement affects all parties involved with ramifications for the future.

This chapter is a theological reflection that seeks to raise questions regarding the interaction of language and the creation of communal and personal identity. First, I examine the diversity and role of languages within the context of Latin@ lived experiences in the United States as this affects world views and self-perception of Hispanics, youth in particular. Second, I explore relationships among language, identity, and culture specifically through the concrete experiences of a sector of the U.S. Latin@ community that remains our own marginalized minority, Hispanic Deaf and the hearing children of Latin@ deaf couples.[5] Third, I propose directions that arise from these encounters with hopes for further theological reflection that might inform pastoral practice.

## LIVING LA LENGUA COTIDIANA

Linguistic diversity among U.S. Latin@s is far more complicated and emotionally and politically charged than bilingual paradigms suggest. Language and the use of language have become the litmus test of one's latinidad. While, ideally, many see the value of maintaining fluency and literacy in more than one language (a hope shared by numbers of Latin American and Spanish immigrants seeking opportunities in the United States), the implied U.S. cultural norm is conveyed in the monolingual primacy of English. "Language difference, after all, is still a prime marker of identity for Latino communities and is equivocally addressed within the English monoglot terrain of the United States."[6]

Language preferences and abilities, not necessarily predicated by age, range from Spanish dominance to English dominance with an assortment in between. However, for the most part, the discourse is characterized in binary (Spanish/English) or hybrid terms (Spanglish). As the Dame Edna incident reveals, the Spanish language has maintained a presence beyond any symbolic longing for a romanticized past. Spanish has endured through first and second generations, unlike many other immigrants' languages, in part because of the ease in maintaining transnational relationships and identities with Latin America. Spanish has secured a visible presence in the United States, and it should be noted that the designation "foreign" for Spanish seems odd, considering that its presence in the Americas, for better or worse, predates the arrival of English, and it remains an official and the dominant language of Puerto Rico—a part of the U.S. colonial constellation. Spanish carries economic capital and maintains a market influence, as the Condé Nast publishing group certainly learned: "As Californios and Floridians say in Spanglish: Hacer enojar a muchos Latinos con laptops puede ser peligroso."[7] The consumer power of Latin@s fuels a marketing industry that is "directly involved in the maintenance of latinidad's Hispanic core through its economically driven need to emphasize the permanence of the Spanish language as the basis for Latino/Hispanic identity to ensure and perpetuate its own existence and profitability."[8] Commercial representation and marketing are "still predicated on the idea that there is an untainted ethnic base that can be sold and projected in the media and that it is language that provides the greatest variable for defining Latinos' cultural identity."[9]

On the other hand, in the music industry the success and presence in hip-hop of English-speaking Latino rappers cautions against overemphasizing and/or oversimplifying the relationship between language and cultural identity. The preference for English in the raps of a number of second-, third-, and fourth-generation U.S. Latin@s reveals both a comfort level with English and a solidarity with the medium's Afro-diasporic roots and fan base.

> The assumption that the use of English by Latino rappers equals Anglocentrism whereas the use of Spanish or bilingualism signals some kind of adherence to Latinidad points to severe conceptual problems. Equating the use of English with Anglocentrism negates the appropriation and transformation of the colonizers' language by Afro-diasporic people. Besides, not only are Latinos following Afro-diasporic English-based orality, but their use of English also derives from their most immediate communicative experience as young people raised in the United States. . . . Puerto Ricans, as well as other Latinos, frequently assert their cultural identity through their particular way of speaking English.[10]

Illustrating the complexity of the U.S. Latin@ relationship with languages, Nuyorican poet Martín Espada borrows an analogy from his friend, another New York Puerto Rican writer, Jack Agüeros: "English and Spanish are like two dogs I love. English is an obedient dog. When I tell him to sit, he sits. Spanish is a disobedient dog. When I tell him to sit, he pees on the couch."[11] While this amusing image expresses differences in command between a first and a second language, the other perros in the litter (the so-called hybrids) are left out. For some, especially in the younger generations, Spanglish[12] offers a voice that holds in creative tension the multiple dimensions of hybrid identities. This linguistic border crossing, or codeswitching, occurs often in the same sentence. In a "move to trilingualism," Spanglish, in its many forms, demonstrates that today Spanish (and I would add English) is "as elastic and polyphonic as ever, allowing for a wide gamut of voices that goes beyond mere localisms."[13] For some, Spanglish is a reaction, a cultural resistance to assimilation in a nation that prizes monolinguality, especially as a ticket to success.[14] For others, "Spanglish también is often an intra-ethnic vehicle of communication, though only in Unaited Esteits . . . to establish a form of empathy between one another . . . a result of the evident clash between two full-fledged, perfectly discernible lenguas; and it is not defined by class, as people in all social strata . . . use it regularly."[15] Neither is it defined by age as usage crosses generational lines as well. "One only has to ride the New York City subway . . . to witness clusters of young Latinos skillfully and expressively codeswitching among their multilingual and multidialectical speech repertoire without dropping a beat. This linguistic vibrancy evinces how the city's Latino youth have become accomplished linguistic practitioners."[16]

As life on the ever-changing linguistic borders illustrates, identities and the networks within which they are created and rene-gotiated are dynamic and fluid. Vida cotidiana counters what Seyla Benhabib calls the "false assumptions about cultures, their coherence and purity." Instead, daily living affirms "recognition of the radical hybridity and polyvocality of all cultures; cultures themselves, as well as societies, are not holistic but polyvocal, multilayered, decentered, and fractured systems of action and signification."[17] Living la lengua cotidiana reveals the power struggles at work in all human interactions and betrays the dichotomy between margins and center, insider and outsider. Language as a turf marker or border establishes who belongs and who does not; it excludes as much as it includes. In the words of Fernando Segovia:

> We are a people who live in two worlds, but find ourselves at home in neither one. . . . We share a world of the past, but we do so with many homes, many mixtures, many traditions, and many conceptions of reality. We further share a world of the present, but again, we do so with many faces, many histories, and many visions of God and the world. We are thus not only a bicultural people but a multicultural people, the permanent others who are also in various respects others to one another.[18]

## IN THIS SIGN:
## LO COTIDIANO ON THE LINGUISTIC MARGINS

In *Freak*, his autobiographical one-man Broadway show, Latino comedian John Leguizamo introduces his uncle Sanny in his pantheon of characters. Described by Leguizamo as his "surrogate moms," Sanny was "a little unconventional . . . what you'd call a triple threat: Latin, gay and deaf."[19] Sanny, using his Spanglish ASL,[20] illustrates the deeper complexity of the U.S. comunidad latina. On the linguistic margins, Hispanic Deaf persons and the hearing children of Deaf Latin@ parents further nuance an already complicated relationship in the triad of language-identity-culture. By their very existence Hispanic Deaf people threaten assumptions that ground a binary linguistic construction of culture and identity.

Living on the margins of our Hispanic marginality, this community of Deaf people and the hearing children of Deaf parents bears witness that orality and aurality are unfairly privileged in the construction of communal identity. Sign Language interpreter Maria Izaguirre describes a coming of age "as confused, mixed, and multi-cultural as the one Leguizamo acts out in *Freak*." She further elaborates:

> I had a pot-luck kind of early life. Both my parents were deaf. I grew up thinking all parents were deaf. I began using sign language when I was a year old. I learned English backwards. My father was Mexican and my mother Puerto Rican. So I had signing in Spanish, signing in English, the deaf community and the hearing Mexican community, all mixed together. Like John, I had an early self-identity crisis. I had to sort it all out in my adult life.[21]

According to the Census Bureau statistics for 2000, Hispanics are the fastest growing minority group in the United States, a community marked by its ethnic diversity and the overwhelming youth of its population. Left out of these statistics is the reality that Hispanics also constitute the fastest-growing ethnic group among deaf students, in part due to immigration from Mexico, Central America, and the Caribbean. A growing number of Latin@ Deaf youth come from Spanish-dominant homes and are among the first generation in their families to attend school and live in the United States. Unlike previous generations of U.S. Deaf, yet like many of their youthful deaf peers, the majority of Hispanic Deaf children are not in residential educational settings but in mainstream programs. However, for Latin@s the reason appears to be that their parents do not want them far from family and "do not want to transfer the child-rearing responsibilities to other parties."[22] This emphasis on familia has both positive and negative ramifications: "On one hand their families overprotect them from the dangers of the world. At the same time, they make them feel left out of vital discussions and family decisions."[23]

Immigrant deaf people and the deaf children of Spanish-speaking families face the daunting challenge of learning multiple new languages and cultures in the United States, as well as "Hispanic Deaf culture, which is learned from older students and Hispanic Deaf adults."[24] Entering school using sign languages unknown by their U.S. teachers, "the school may label these immigrant children as having 'no language,' rather than as using a different language. . . . Their language differences are seen as a disability."[25]

Too many Deaf Latin@s, in particular the young, are left straddling multiple worlds of disconnection with no place to stand. As the overwhelming majority of deaf children are born to hearing parents, they are cut off in many ways from the oral tradition in Hispanic cultures expressed through storytelling, dichos, and so on, that transmit cultural identity. In other words, Deaf Latin@s are "immersed in the culture, but not enmeshed."[26] Born of hearing parents and educated in mainstream programs in which hearing students outnumber deaf students, many Deaf Latin@s navigate their world through interpreters. They become outsiders to the daily interactions most take for granted. In some ways they are removed from experiences of Deaf culture in the United States, a culture where language, American Sign Language (ASL), also plays a defining role in the formation and understanding of identity. For Deaf Latin@s in the U.S. context, the languages of discourse are American Sign Language and English, with an emphasis on its written expression, while the language of the home is often Spanish. The intimate relationship of sign languages, identity, and Deaf culture are evident not only in the United States, but increasingly in Latin America as members of this linguistic minority shift the discourse from issues of ability/disability to communication and human rights.[27]

## OTHERCIDE OR OTHER SIDE: LESSONS IN BORDER CROSSINGS

othercide (oh-THER-sayd), n., m., the elimination of people or attributes different to us or ours.[28]

A refreshing feature of the theologies emerging from U.S. Latin@ perspectives is a willingness to admit that our reflections are situated and engaged, dependent on and interdependent with "certain communities of discourse, and certain 'webs of interlocution.'"[29] At the same time we recognize that in order to keep "the circle of discourse from degenerating into monologue, cross-contextual conversations can help to prevent the celebration of bias from trapping interpreters in their own ghettos of private meaning."[30] My reflection on the implications of linguistic diversity in la comunidad latina, and some directions it suggests for further theological reflection and pastoral practice, are very much shaped by my own social location. Languages matter to me. They are precious inheritances passed between and across generations. As a second-generation U.S. citizen I struggle to regain the fluency I once had as a child in Spanish, la lengua de mi abuela. Spanish is a living link to my beloved Nana, who passed away too early in my youth, and Spanglish increasingly characterizes my daily interactions. ASL is the language I learned in adolescence at the hands of New York's Deaf Catholics, both junior and senior to me, and the dedicated hearing priest who has accompanied this community for almost forty years. It remains, like so many youthful explorations, a border crossing with life-altering consequences.

Theological reflection on the implications of linguistic diversity in U.S. Hispanic communities raises broader questions about how we deal with difference and commonality with respect to the networks that form and inform us as individuals and as communities. How do we not sacrifice our differences in attempts to relate on common ground while building alliances across constituencies of marginalization? How do we address the reality that these alliances must also exist entre nosotros? First, and painfully, we must admit that marginalized communities can and do marginalize others within their own groups. Reflecting on his experiences as a Deaf Latino, educator Angel Ramos observed:

People who have been oppressed tend to oppress others, and that is why there is so much oppression even within our own communities. As a Deaf person or as a Hispanic person I just never felt that oppression growing up in NYC. It wasn't until I arrived at Gallaudet that I felt that oppression as a Hispanic, it wasn't until I arrived in Texas that I felt that oppression as a Deaf person.[31]

As communities of faith, how we respond to these questions determines our ability to survive across generations. Do we continue practices of othercide, or do we model the type of crossings to the other side that ground productive and healthy coalitions?

Exploring the linguistic diversity that marks U.S. Hispanic experiences, in cross-cultural conversation with U.S. Deaf experiences, suggests the following factors that need to be considered in developing effective strategies for theological and pastoral border crossing.

## INTRAGENERATIONAL TRADITIONING

The significance of intragenerational traditioning is especially evident in Deaf communities because the overwhelming majority of deaf people are born to hearing parents. Therefore, the Deaf "make up the only cultural group where cultural information and language has been *predominantly* passed down from child to child rather than from adult to child."[32] This experience increasingly marks daily living among Hispanic immigrants both deaf and hearing. In the early generations in particular, the young transition each other influenced by multiple relationships besides family. Attention to transmission within a generation does not mean diminishing the value of transgenerational traditioning. The challenge for theologians and ministers is to reflect more intentionally on both means, especially considering the significant role of familia in las vidas latinas and the ongoing concern for a population characterized by the predominance of young people.

## COALITIONS AMONG MARGINALIZED COMMUNITIES

Border crossing calls for coalition building across marginalized communities in order to secure justice. We must take care to avoid the temptation to downsize "justice for all" into the more manageable "justice for some" in efforts to advance our own particular agendas. Sadly, solidarity has been compromised and justice postponed too frequently. The familiar refrain, "first we'll get x, then we'll come back for you," has unfortunately marked movements from abolition to women's suffrage to civil rights.

Deaf Latin@s challenge the greater U.S. Deaf community to recognize and address its own diversity. The emerging use of the term *bicultural* to describe Deaf experience as being affected by interactions in both Deaf and hearing worlds certainly resonates with the "life on the hyphen" experience of many U.S. Latin@s. From a Deaf perspective, Carol Padden suggests that "to talk of the 'bicultural' is not to talk about an additive state, to be of two cultures, but more about states of tensions."[33] Padden proposes "the term 'bicultural' is being used to describe a way of conceiving boundaries between Deaf and hearing people in a world where the residential schools and the Deaf clubs of the past no longer exist."[34] As these familiar institutions of deaf life changed or disappeared, Padden observes, "middle-class professional Deaf people began to imagine new ways of representing themselves, largely in the form of calls for cultural ways of living and bicultural schools and workplaces."[35]

However, as a growing transcultural population stretches the boundaries of U.S. Deaf culture, Barbara Gerner de Garcia expresses concern that the Deaf community's battle for recognition as bilingual and bicultural may cause some within the Deaf community to view "multiculturalism as another battle that might divert attention from their own struggle."[36] She reminds both Deaf and hearing people, Latin@s and non-Latin@s, that "ignoring the multicultural and multilingual nature of the Deaf Community negatively impacts multicultural members of the Deaf Community, particularly immigrant deaf students."[37]

Deaf Latin@s challenge the privileging of orality and aurality in the creation of la comunidad latina in the United States, and this raises questions about what constitutes a particularly Hispanic issue. For example, in the Archdiocese of New York, the Deaf community was in danger of losing the Manhattan parish that has housed Deaf ministry for a number of years. St. Elizabeth of Hungary Church serves two congregations, hearing Catholics who live within its territorial boundaries and Deaf Catholics who come from throughout the Archdiocese of New York and the Diocese of Brooklyn. This church is also a meeting site for Deaf groups including the Puerto Rican Society for the Catholic Deaf and the Black Deaf Advocates. In the face of shifting priorities and dwindling resources, there was a risk of this church closing, a victim of reorganization. While archdiocesan officials promised that the ministry would survive, they could not guarantee where it would be located.[38]

The archdiocesan failure to comprehend the significance of having one's own space should not be lost on Hispanic congregations. The basements of our own churches have too often been home to the Spanish-language services. The fact that the majority of the New York Deaf affected by the archdiocesan decision are Puerto Rican and Dominican raises a further question: Is this just a Deaf concern, or is it also a Latin@ issue?

Explorations of our multiple belongings and their impact on the development of identity and community may provide common ground and illuminate concomitant responsibilities to justice.


## LANGUAGE, COMMUNITY, AND RESISTANCE

In the public forum language can serve as bridge in the construction of identity, collective and personal, or, as a privileging of aural ability and oral expression demonstrate, it can cut others off from conversation. Sensitivity to this dynamic begins with the realization that vocabulary matters too. Carelessness with

language is antithetical to coalition building. For example, constant references to "voice" in justice discourse, the use of deaf-
ness, usually in preaching to express a spiritual void, and the
assumption of hearing as a precondition for acceptance of the
"word," all serve to create distance and to imply a misguided,
divine preference for communication dependent upon a physical, auditory modality.

Language is created by community and in turn facilitates the
creation of community. For example, amid overwhelming efforts
by hearing educators to enforce oralism,[39] religious ministries
and Deaf churches played a historic role in preserving sign language and in traditioning Deaf youth. Hearing clergy learned at
the hands of Deaf sign-language masters, and Deaf ministers as
well as adult Deaf congregants served as role models for children whose schoolteachers were predominantly non-signing,
hearing people. Susan Burch writes:

> Addressing the Deaf in a public venue like a church de-
> manded a masterful command of Sign Language. . . . The
> signing ability of ministers aided the preservation of Sign
> Language in the twentieth century, for most ministers to
> the Deaf had ample access to preach at state schools. . . .
> The message was essential to the religious education and
> the medium unified the culture.[40]

From ASL to Spanglish, language creates a discursive space.
Ironically, both Spanish and ASL have suffered at the hands of
"English only" protagonists. Yet, they have endured as languages
that are more indigenous to the U.S. experience than they are
foreign. This power of language to create community also fosters agency. Douglas Baynton writes:

> So long as deaf people had their own language and com-
> munity, they possessed a cultural space in which to create
> alternative meanings for their lives. They could resist the
> meanings that hearing people attached to deafness, adopt

them and put them to new uses, or create their own . . .
because deaf people themselves chose not to relinquish the
autonomous cultural space that their community and language made possible.[41]

From this perspective of language as resistance, inclusion rhetoric is a manifestation of assimilation, not border crossing. This
is a concern shared by constituencies who reside on the margins.
Robert Schreiter cautiously observes, "Inclusion touches upon
the deepest human yearnings for belonging. But if inclusion means
a complete erasure of difference, does it still remain an ideal?"[42]
Sometimes as theologians, ministers, and people of faith, we
are tempted to embrace inclusion paradigms naively, believing
that only positive interpretations can exist. Careful attention to
lo cotidiano reveals alternate perspectives. In the case of Deaf
people, Baynton explains, "In the name of inclusion in 'the' community, deaf children are frequently denied inclusion in any community. For the sake of an abstraction known as the 'mainstream,'
deaf children are denied the solid and tangible fellowship, culture, language and heritage of the deaf community."[43] In such
contexts, inclusion—whether understood as melting pot or as
mainstream—is merely assimilation. It signifies loss not liberation, isolation not community. This is an unfortunate experience
shared by too many individuals and communities who reside on
the margins of what is considered to be normative.
Katherine Jankowski describes how in ASL, the sign for
mainstreaming presents a visual rendering of what could best be
described as mutual integration, left hand down fingers spread
moving toward right hand in the same configuration. The result
gives an impression of integration, an encounter of mutuality,
where each digit and hand still maintains its own integrity. However, the experience of mainstreaming betrays hidden assumptions, Jankowski explains: "Once Deaf people are placed among
their hearing peers, they will learn to read and write English flu-
ently, to speak and hear."[44] In response to this experience another

sign was created, in mockery, reflecting not opportunity but oppression, or as we say in Spanglish, othercide. In this sign, Jankowski describes, only the index finger on the right hand moves toward the open five of the left, this time the image is not one of mutual exchange in the context of integrity, but of "only one Deaf person in the midst of a mass of hearing people, and the Deaf person is subordinately squashed."[45] In many ways this image and experience parallels what Ada María Isasi-Díaz calls "one-way traveling" as opposed to genuine border crossing:

> The lack of knowledge and appreciation of marginalized cultures makes world-traveling mostly a one way affair, because Latinas and Latinos are not allowed to bring into the dominant construction of the world elements from our own culture. It is also a one-way traveling because the few people of the dominant group who travel to our world insist on changing it by acting in the Latina world the way they act in theirs.[46]

A common hope emerges as U.S. Hispanic communities struggle to embrace the complexities of pan-Latin@ diversity and as a once bicultural/bilingual U.S. Deaf community seeks to understand itself in light of a new transnational multilingual reality. Perhaps one day soon individuals will be able to move back and forth across borders "with a minimum of interference and without the concomitant discomforts of marginality."[47]

The presence and daily lived experiences of our Hispanic Deaf and their hearing familia invite our respective communities to explore common ground in la lucha for justice. Failure by our communities to recognize Deaf Latin@s entails a risk of creating a condition of permanent otherness. Failure by our communities to engage en conjunto with our Deaf hermanos y hermanas leaves us all, in various respects, strangers still to one another. We need to cultivate an appreciation for the reality that we do not toil alone. If we take seriously our engagement with the stories and contexts of others' lived experiences, especially those others who are also us, then we must be prepared to travel outside our own narrow contexts and venture into possible zones of discomfort— only then will we cross borders.

The intersection and transmission of language and tradition create a dynamic exchange that in each generation inevitably births new possibilities and interpretations. These language matters invite the U.S. church to navigate the tension of respecting particularity while retaining unity, of being a community of inclusion but not assimilation. Without sustained reflection on language as a source of our theologizing, and as a component of community and identity, diversity will be perceived as an obstruction to unity and a challenge for ministry.

# 6

# ¡Cuidado! The Church Who Cares and Pastoral Hostility

The church can regard no one as excluded from its motherly embrace, no one as outside the scope of its motherly care.

—PAUL VI, *ECCLESIAM SUAM*

When asked by my scholarly colleagues to identify my theological method, I sometimes half jokingly reply, "pastoral hostility." While this response draws a nervous chuckle from the academic side of the house, the very same response resonates deeply among the pastoral agents with whom I have shared it. When I mentioned my unique methodological insight at a gathering of Latin@s involved in professional ministries across the United States, they did not laugh. Rather, they expressed gratitude because this paradoxical expression had somehow managed to articulate what we were experiencing daily in our respective ministries. My colleagues asked for clarification and immediately appropriated the phrase into Spanish, deciding that hostilidad pastoral was the oxymoron that best suited the reality of our ministries.

While pastoral hostility may appear to be a contradiction in terms, in light of the signs of our times and the struggles manifest in the lived experiences of the varied peoples we accompany, it should come as no surprise that our ability to care may at times be compromised by frustration, loss, fear, and even anger. As ministers, how do we care in contexts of unfathomable injustice? How can we be present, especially when suffering seems senseless? How do we accompany communities where cycles of poverty, violence, or indifference appear impenetrable? How do we navigate the borders of faith and politics?

The signs of our ecclesial times are equally disturbing. The closings and/or mergings of Catholic parishes and schools raise painful questions about our commitments, especially to our own most vulnerable and poor neighbors. The streamlining of personnel in diocesan and parish ministries and the sagging morale of clergy and religious cannot be easily extricated from the billion dollars plus paid in settlements. As a church and as ministers, how do we survive the current crisis in confidence that years of abuse, cover-up, and mismanagement have created? How do we recover financially in order to provide the quality of care our communities deserve? How do we labor with inadequate resources, limited institutional support, and competing needs? As pastoral ministers, how do we go on? As church, why should we care?

The expression *pastoral hostility* can remind us that anger may be stagnating and paralyzing. Anger can stunt creativity, and quite frankly, it has not been an emotion that those whose profession calls for compassion are encouraged to express, let alone admit. Yet anger can be constructive as well; it can serve as impetus for necessary change, if, in the words of the poet Martín Espada, this anger is "controlled, directed, creatively channeled, articulated but not all consuming, neither destructive nor self-destructive."[1] In the midst of all that aggravates and cries out for redress, how do ministers continue to ensure basic levels of care within our communities? How do we care as ministers, as people of faith, without losing ourselves, without forgetting the hope that animates our passion? As church, why must we care? If we neglect this fundamental aspect of our identity and mission, will we risk fostering attitudes of indifference, a collective and exasperated "Whatever! Who cares?"

## THE ROOTS OF PASTORAL CARE

Pastoral care can be traced to the earliest days of the nascent communities of post-resurrection Jesus-followers. In his earliest letter, to the Thessalonians, Paul recounts the posture with which the gospel and its ministers encountered their community: "We were gentle among you, like a nurse tenderly caring for her own children. So deeply do we care for you that we are determined to share with you not only the gospel of God but also our own selves, because you have become very dear to us" (1 Thes 2:7–8). Initially a responsibility of the apostles, care for the spiritual and material needs of emerging communities soon required the engagement of others. In the Acts of the Apostles, tension between Greek-speaking and Aramaic-speaking Jewish Jesus-followers is manifest in complaints that Hellenist widows are being neglected in the daily distribution of food. Therefore, the community selects seven members to assume the responsibility of feeding the hungry (Acts 6:1–6).

In the Corinthian community, expanding needs and the tensions that accompany growth are expressed in terms of a diversity of ministerial roles providing for spiritual, physical, and material care: "And God has appointed in the church first apostles, second prophets, third teachers; then deeds of power, then gifts of healing, forms of assistance, forms of leadership, various kinds of tongues" (1 Cor 12:28).

The community itself was also charged with the responsibility of caring, as the first letter of Peter reminds it: "Above all, maintain constant love for one another, for love covers a multitude of sins. Be hospitable to one another without complaining. Like good stewards of the manifold grace of God, serve one another with whatever gift each of you has received" (1 Pt 4:8–10). Caring extended across communities; Acts records the sending of relief in time of famine from Antioch, via Barnabas and Saul, to believers in Judea (Acts 11:28–30).

A journey through New Testament texts reveals caring that was contextual, practical, and concerned for the everyday. The earliest disputes betray the tensions associated with contextualized care that sought to address the particularity of communities diversified by religion, language, geography, culture, social, and economic factors. The practical aspects of care were not ignored, as is evident in the gospel accounts of feeding and healing in the ministry of Jesus and in the ministry of the early communities of Jesus' followers. From the beginning they were aware that ministry occurred in the accompaniment of individuals and communities within daily living. Concern for daily life in its ordinariness as well as its struggles comes through in exhortations and encouragement on everything from familial and spousal relations to survival and steadfastness amidst persecution. Retrieving New Testament images invites us to reconsider care as a constitutive component of ministry with attention to its contextual dimensions, exercised within the course of our daily living.

## THE SHAPE OF PASTORAL CARE

Care remains a defining characteristic of pastoral ministry. How care is understood is open to interpretation, and this is reflected in the variety of constructions across Christian denominations. In the Roman Catholic tradition, *cura animarum* (care of souls) is intertwined with a sacramental dimension. In light of contemporary challenges facing sacramental ministry, present circumstances call for a shift from models that focus on the minister, usually ordained, as provider of care, to ministry as a network of caring professionals and resources. In turn, the local faith community becomes a locus of care, not just a collection of supplicants in need.

The traditional functions of care are formulated in terms of guiding, sustaining, healing, and reconciling individuals and communities. In recent years, thanks to the influence of feminist, liberationist, and contextual theologies, these functions have been expanded to include nurturing, supporting, and discerning, as well as resisting, empowering, and liberating. African American pastoral theologians have also reminded us that caring sometimes cannot proceed to liberation when basic survival is at stake.

## CARING IS CONTEXTUAL

Like theology, pastoral ministry is local and contextual. Ministry as a process of accompaniment is necessarily contextual, as it entails attending to particular individuals and communities, in particular times and circumstances, with particular needs, gifts, challenges, and limitations. Following a June 1998 dialogue on lay ministry, with ecclesial counterparts from across the Americas, an adviser for the host U.S. bishops' subcommittee observed: "In many ways, ministry is culture-specific." This observation followed conversation "about the class affluence differences of a faith and church brought by conquerors or immigrants, stability or mobility; poverty or middle, valuing of relationships and community or of individualism and independence."[2]

It may seem obvious that differences in social location call for a plurality of pastoral responses. Recognizing the contextuality of care challenges us as ministers and as local church to question assumptions of universality that disguise our particularity. Ghanaian pastoral theologian Emmanuel Lartey cautions:

> Pastoral care is dependent upon the cultures, reigning philosophies, and psychologies of the periods in which it is practiced. Forms of pastoral care and counseling practiced in Western societies in the twentieth century and now the twenty-first reflect the dominant social, cultural, theological, and psychological theories of the West. There are real differences between theories and practices of effective pastoral care and counseling in different parts of the globe.[3]

Such diversity is not only a global matter, but also part of the context of life in the United States. As pastoral care gradually moves to inculturation from therapeutic paradigms that have only recently acknowledged the impact of contextual factors, strategies are necessary to uncover the hidden presuppositions that guide pastoral responses while allowing local contexts to dictate direction.

In his book *Jesus Weeps* pastor and theologian Harold Recinos recommends what he calls "pastoral anthropology" as a means for providing ecclesial communities with contextual understanding of the dynamics operative within their own experience of local church.[4] The types of questions he suggests and the level of observation he proposes invite theological reflection and informed practical engagement and raise individual and communal "critical understanding of the social dimensions of systems of oppression that structure human experience each day everywhere."[5] If caring is contextual, then exploration of the relationship of a church to its neighborhood is as necessary as attention to the ordering of the church's physical space. Which ministries are funded, which community worships in the basement, what languages we use—all these say something about our priorities. The accessibility of our common spaces and our worship space sends a message about who is welcome, who can participate, and who can exercise liturgical roles in the assembly. From the connection between ritual life and theological identity to the social structure of parish leadership, all aspects deserve local analysis because they reveal not only who belongs, but also who is left on the margins. This type of ministerial and communal introspection can lay bare dysfunction and abuse of power and at the same time highlight efforts that mark a community as faithful to its mission.

Encouraging ministers and communities to reflect on their own particularity as it is expressed in their social and ritual lives, their physical space, and their interpersonal and professional relationships focuses caring on the local context in a given time. This process can serve as a corrective to well-intentioned yet misguided efforts to address diversity in pastoral settings. For example, in some situations the rapid growth in the number of Hispanic Catholics in the United States has resulted in a pan-Latinization of particular experiences and symbols (such as Our Lady of Guadalupe). We need to ask ourselves who makes such symbols normative, who are the evangelizers? Are these the things our peoples really think about, or are they made normative because we as theologians and ministers choose to promote them? Do our attempts at sensitivity impose a monolithic culture on a presence whose diversity defies simple categorization by race, class, nationality, language, and expression of popular religion?

## CARING IN LO COTIDIANO

If pastoral care is contextual, then daily living emerges as a privileged source of theological reflection and the locus of our ministerial praxis. In the words of mujerista theologian Ada-María Isasi-Díaz, "Lo cotidiano makes social location explicit, for it is the context of the person in relation to physical space, ethnic space, social space."[6] Daily living cannot be reduced simply to the private or domestic sphere. As Orlando Espín points out: "It might be argued that the so-called macro or public sphere only influences people's lives if, when, and to the degree that it existentially affects them at the daily or micro level. It may be conversely argued that there is ultimately no real-life substance or consistency to the macro sphere. Real life exists in the concrete, the local, the familial and communal, the micro."[7]

Refocusing pastoral ministry on la vida cotidiana counters the temptation to construct the function of care narrowly. The daily aspect of ministry challenges tendencies to view care and counseling primarily in terms of intervention in times of crisis. Care entails dealing with the ordinary: the tedious, the crises, the struggles, the joys, moments of passage, and the mundane.

Sometimes it requires extensive pastoral planning, and other times the only appropriate response is to accept that there is nothing one can do or say except to be present.

Engaging in the messiness of daily living empowers ministers and communities to seek the transformation of injustice in the public as well as the domestic arenas. The daily focuses a spotlight on the ravages of poverty, the destruction of addiction, the paralysis of abuse, and the tolls of racism, sexism, homophobia, and xenophobia. In the daily, one comprehends the public role of pastoral ministry. Hospital and nursing-home visitations raise questions about the affordability of health care and the complexity of biomedical issues. The wages of war come home when local churches bury military personnel who have died in Iraq and Afghanistan. In the daily living of our ministries we learn humbling and painful lessons: justice takes time; we cannot heal, save, reconcile, or liberate everyone, but we are obligated to care. María Pilar Aquino provides perspective:

> Theologically, daily life has salvific value because the people themselves, in *lo cotidiano* of their existence, let us experience the salvific presence of God here and now in their daily struggles for humanization, for a better quality of life, and for greater social justice. At the same time, daily life urges us to join actively in the long march toward a new humanity and a future of fulfillment still latent in the heart of creation, until we reach God's definitive salvation.[8]

The "long march toward a new humanity" begins in the very practical steps taken in la vida cotidiana. Pope John Paul II observed, "What are needed are everyday gestures, done with simplicity and constancy; that are capable of producing an authentic change in interpersonal relationships."[9] The latest waves of immigration to the United States illustrate the need for care that is contextual and immersed in the daily. The complexities of immigration can obscure the reality that national policies affect the daily living of actual, situated human beings, our neighbors, our kin, and our parishioners. Focus on the magnitude of migration conceals the reality that "the work of welcome is practical but not easy."[10] Addressing migration as church requires an appreciation for theology as local[11] and welcome as practical, intentional, and daily. In the words of Bishop Nicholas DiMarzio of Brooklyn: "If you think we can avoid that type of street-to-street work and still serve the newcomers, you're wrong. We need to use personal contact to overcome resistance at times and we need to reach out to people who are sometimes very isolated and often frightened and suspicious."[12]

On the other hand, engaging migration on a daily basis reminds us that for the church, the local is also global. Our documented and alternately documented parishioners, "on account of the peculiarly universal nature of the church, are not outsiders."[13] An earthquake in El Salvador influences the Archdiocese of Washington, civil unrest in Haiti affects the Archdiocese of Miami, the "church of departure" and the "church of arrival" are bound to each other and obligated to "keep up their own pastoral responsibility in light of a lively and practically expressed feeling of reciprocity."[14] As a continent, at the national level of episcopal conferences, we are connected; on a local level, church to church, we remain strangers to each other.

## EN CONJUNTO

As a response to the signs of the times, pastoral hostility/ hostilidad pastoral discloses the prophetic dimension of care. It harkens back to the images of the Old Testament prophets, whose righteous rage was fueled by a hope that what is unjust must no longer be and will not be in God's own time. Prophets see what is and cajole communities to be what they should be because prophets are grounded in their communities and are invested in their care. But even prophetic ministers need to be aware of the temptation to lose sight of the people whom they accompany in their struggles.

Even with the best of intentions, we too can participate or collude in the process of silencing those we seek to uphold, ignoring the dignity we share. For example, a tour of an Immigration and Naturalization Service detention camp on the El Paso/Juarez border made its way through the medical clinic. The "tourists" were theologians, their guide a hardworking chaplain, the current attraction an examining room with a gregarious and dedicated medical professional. A young man sat in plain sight on an examining table with a thermometer in his mouth, invisible and voiceless. He appeared to be no more than a teenager, nameless even to those who were most committed to justice at the borders. The conversation swirled in English around a patient whose violated privacy went unnoticed. Finally, a sheepish introduction was initiated, and the long overdue question asked, "Lo siento, me llamo . . . . ¿Como se llama usted?"

Ministry as a process of accompaniment in la vida cotidiana of particular contexts is not a solo process: it is mutual. As a U.S. Hispanic theologian and pastoral minister, my praxis—which includes my teaching and scholarship—is influenced by the necessary interrelationship between teología en conjunto and pastoral en conjunto. The premise is that theology and pastoral activity are communal endeavors that require mutual engagement and accountability. Such a posture values experience as a locus theologicus and builds upon critical, reflective interaction between the practical and the theoretical, an integration of the scholarly with the grassroots. Engagement accomplished en conjunto—that is, together, within community—recognizes the need to cross borders while respecting the integrity of boundaries. Fruitful relationships grow in contexts of gracious hospitality that appreciate that when we are in each other's company we are on sacred ground.

From the perspective of teología y pastoral de conjunto, pastoral theology emerges as the primordial contextual theology whose analysis cannot be divorced from daily lived experience or from conscientious involvement in pastoral practice.

# 7

# Elbows on the Table

## The Complex Contexts of lo popular

Metaphors and narratives are multivalent, and how one understands relates to one's experience and social location. The feminist critique of God-language, for example, uncovered the paternalism, patriarchy, and kyriarchy imbued in terms like *Father* and *Lord*. However, addressing God as Parent or even Mother does not resolve the problem. Not all of us share the same experiences of parenthood or of being parented, and the same holds true for the metaphor *table*. While frequently used, it cannot be assumed that we share a common understanding or even a universal, let alone positive experience of the table. Three experiences of table ground and shape my understanding: a noisy chorizo-filching familia, eighteen years of high school cafeterias, and years of ACHTUS colloquia. Within each of these contexts the need to have one's elbows firmly planted on the table emerges as essential for engagement, if not survival.

Some of my earliest memories are of sitting around the dinner table with my parents and siblings, and my favorite occasions are those where our family gathers around the same table for holidays, celebrations, or for no particular reason. My most fluent Spanish remains the simple table blessing taught to us as children by my mother and still faithfully prayed before each meal, especially by my Czech/Slavic American father. All have a seat and a voice at our table from the most senior to the youngest, and the exchanges are noisy and spirited. My poor tía's stories take forever to communicate because her nieces and nephew cannot resist interrupting with embellishments, and bringing up religion or politics is sure to ignite passions. At our very family-oriented table there always appears to be room to include a last-minute or unexpected guest. If empanada gallega[1] happens to be on the menu, every semblance of civility is gone, at least among us now-grown children, as the favored chorizos are liberated from passing or unguarded plates. No matter the meal or the menu, enough food is left over for "nice sandwiches" and "doggy bags" for my brother's dog and cat.

During my years as a high-school religion teacher, campus minister, and administrator, I logged countless hours of cafeteria duty. What I have observed is that lunchtime is too brief, that there is never enough time for interaction and engagement. Some tables are tight and boisterous, and others are strikingly sparse as lonely kids consume their lunches in isolation. High-school cafeterias follow a code of inclusion and exclusion that disturbs adults more than students. Indeed, self-segregation is more often than not perceived by administrators and faculty as a problem. Psychologist Beverly Daniel Tatum raises the question in the title of her book, *Why Are All the Black Kids Sitting Together in the Cafeteria?*, and suggests that it is necessary to understand racial self-segregation within racially diverse settings as a positive coping strategy. "Racial grouping is a developmental process in response to an environmental stressor, racism."[2] I would add that sometimes it is just a reflection of shared experiences, neighborhood friendships, and common interests. The racial and/or ethnic composition of a cafeteria table, because it is so visually apparent, tends to distract attention from the reality that the segregation runs along even deeper lines, such as Latin@ athletes, African American artists, white music lovers, gay computer techies, and so on. For some kids, the cafeteria table is the place where they are free to be themselves; for others, it is a reminder of their loneliness. It is ground zero for all too many fights and an expression of exuberant communal life.

In some ways my experience of ACHTUS colloquia reflects a combination of the familia and cafeteria tables. The gatherings are passionately spirited yet too brief, intentionally exclusive yet necessarily inclusive. The animated bilingual conversation flows continuously, if not boisterously, from meeting table to dining hall table to banquet table and hopefully back to our respective home, communal, academy, and eventually writing tables.

It can be argued that theology done from the perspectives of U.S. Latinas and Latinos has in the past two decades slowly and forcefully edged its way from the marginal "children's table" of the academy, where proponents of so-called dominant theologies perhaps hoped to contain the growing ranks of contextual theologians. It can certainly be argued that to be represented at the table by others is unacceptable, merely to have a place at the table is inadequate, and to tolerate separate and unequal tables is abhorrent and destructive. However, full participation requires room for engagement as well as table manners, as the words of Ada María Isasi-Díaz illustrate:

> Real engagement among theologies and theologians would mean that a multiplicity of methods would be examined, that different social locations would be analyzed, and that the theological praxis of different communities of struggle would become intrinsic to theological education. Engagement among different theologies would prevent us from falling into total relativity and individualism since all engagement is, in a sense, a calling to accountability. . . . Engagement is not a matter of convincing the other but rather a matter of contributing elements to be considered when reassessment of thinking is going on.[3]

If in simplest terms epistemology is about how we come to know, then ethics is about how we come to do. Therefore, ethics calls for modeling. It is not enough to talk about ethics; as theologians, our theologies need to reflect our ethical stances. In other words, how we do our respective theologies must be ethical. What, then, does table etiquette look like when it is shaped by firmly planted and fully engaged U.S. Hispanic theological contributions? In creating a more inclusive table, what elements emerge from the reflections and praxis of Latino and Latina theologians that inform an ethical doing of theology?

## FROM BASEBALL TO BÉISBOL:
### *VIDA COTIDIANA* AND GLOBALIZATION

While daily lived experience is accorded foundational significance in theologies by Latin@s, the interaction between lo cotidiano and the forces of globalization remains under-explored. The impact of the global on particular vidas cotidianas, and the shaping of global and local forces as result of these continued encounters, invite further theological reflection and articulation if we hope to avoid abstraction. As María Pilar Aquino notes: "The abstraction made of daily life also appears in the priority given to the transformation of the global socioeconomic structures, while overlooking the changes that ought to take place in daily life. This in turn has caused a deviation in the understanding of reality, underestimating the transforming potential found in the personal and private arena."[4]

Daily life may indeed be where transformation takes place, and needs to take place, but how is daily life transformed by globalizing influences and how are globalizing forces affected by the particularities of lo cotidiano? Globalization is not a disembodied process; the changes it brings "wield a powerful impact on everyday life, transforming gender roles, exacerbating generational conflicts, and limiting and creating possibilities for community life."[5] On the other hand, underestimating the power of daily living to affect the global market of goods, ideas, and trends is to ignore the complexity of relationships that are a locus of sin as well as grace. Globalization is "*not* something that occurs *outside* us." Rather, it occurs "within and among all of us, and beyond us,"[6] and its outcomes "are profoundly ambiguous and rife with injustice."[7]

*Time* magazine pop-music critic Christopher John Farley observed, "The first moments of the 21st century have been haunted by the specter of globalization, of a star-spangled world in which a parade of powerful letters—the U.N., the WTO, the IMF—hammers the diversity of the planet into homogenized goop."[8] Absent from his list of powerful acronyms are those letters shaping the lived experience, dreams, and struggles of the young in particular: MTV, AOL, CNN, HBO, WB, NBA, WWF, ESPN, WWW.

A full page ad in the March 20, 2002, edition of the *New York Times,* the week before the beginning of the Major League Baseball season, clearly illustrates that the letters MLB deserve to be added to that list of U.S.-born, influential global acronyms. With text wrapped around a globe/baseball, the ad boasts in quantitative terms that

> Next week people in 224 countries will begin watching an event some people mistakenly call "America's game." In cities all over the world, Major League Baseball will consume the hearts and minds—and inflame the passions of—more people than football, basketball, and hockey put together. . . . By the time the World Series is over, in the United States alone, people will have tuned in to Major League Baseball over 1.5 billion times. . . . In Japan alone, 21 million people will have watched the World Series on TV. In South Africa, 300,000 youngsters play organized baseball.

The ad alludes to the market value of the sport in consumer terms:

> And another 72 million will have spent a memorable afternoon or evening at a ballpark watching Major League

Baseball while devouring 23 million hotdogs, 27 million sodas, and 5 million bags of peanuts.

The ad concludes with an intriguing analysis of baseball's global popularity:

Maybe that's because baseball isn't like any other sport in the world. No, baseball is unique. It transcends languages and countries and cultures. And you don't have to know a darn thing about it to love it. You just have to root, root, root for the home team. Even if that team happens to be in Prague.

The global reach of professional baseball in the twenty-first century was made evident by the opening of the 2000 Major League Baseball season in Japan and the 2001 season in Puerto Rico. If baseball is—as it has been called—the civic religion of the United States,[9] then béisbol may well be a manifestation of popular religion in parts of Latin America. The unprecedented visit of former U.S. president Jimmy Carter to Cuba in May 2002 demonstrates the interrelatedness of baseball and béisbol. If the image of Fidel Castro explaining to Carter the fine art of tossing the first pitch while sharing the mound at the Cuban league All Star game is iconic in its representation of the intersection of globalization and lo cotidiano, then the story of Danny Almonte and the Rolando Paulino All Stars serves as its parable.

In August 2001 the feel-good story of young Danny Almonte, a twelve year old from the Dominican Republic with the arm of a future major leaguer, captivated the sports world. The story contained all the elements of U.S. underdog mythology perpetuated in Disney films: cute, poor kids from the Bronx, the big game, unassuming immigrant hero pursuing the American dream, the purity of sport, evil detractors and jealous opponents with purses large enough to afford private detectives, and the fashionable sabor latino. A media circus surrounded the Bronx Baby

Bombers, as the press dubbed them, and a sponsor-inflated youth event took on big league proportions.

Nevertheless, as with all myths in this postmodern age, deconstruction ruled the day. The twelve-year-old hero became a fourteen-year-old cheater. The detractors were transformed into victims and the cute young immigrants morphed into lying, illegal aliens. The sanctity of a civil religion was blasphemed, and the Little League World Series was revealed to be less about innocent kids enjoying the national pastime than about the creeping corrosiveness, corruption, and greed associated with professional sports.

The controversy surrounding Almonte was framed in markedly ethical terms, though no one could quite agree on the nature of the violation. The debate raged on talk radio and in Internet chatrooms. From the headlines to ESPN, pundits blamed everything from bad parenting to cultural acceptance of lying and cheating in a post-Clinton nation. What most failed to notice was that indeed the pollos of globalization had come home to roost.

Retrieving the long-ignored story of béisbol and the context that framed Almonte's daily lived experience provides an overture for exploring the theological significance of the interaction between vida cotidiana and globalization. This is a necessary first move, inasmuch as baseball is an example of what Robert Schreiter calls a hyperculture, "an overarching cultural proposal that is in itself not a complete culture."[10] Schreiter explains that, influenced and driven by U.S. images and models of consumption, and

> homogenizing as these systems might be, they do not end up homogenizing local cultures altogether. It is increasingly evident that local cultures receive the elements of the hyperculture and reinterpret them in some measure. . . . In other instances, the products of the hyperculture foster a certain cosmopolitanism, a sense of participating in

something larger, grander, and more powerful than our immediate situation.[11]

## FORGOTTEN STORIES

The encounter between baseball and Latin America begins in the 1860s. Brought to Cuba by a variety of means—including students returning from study in U.S. colleges, sailors, those involved in commerce—the game spread rapidly from the docks to the sugar mills, from the elites to the streets, from Cuba throughout the Spanish-speaking Caribbean. Pedro Julio Santana puts the experience in terms theologians can understand:

> It is much the same as that which happened with Christianity. Jesus could be compared to the North Americans, but the apostles were the ones who spread the faith, and the apostles of baseball were the Cubans, they went out into the world to preach the gospel of baseball. Even though the Dominican Republic and Puerto Rico were occupied by the North Americans, the Cubans brought baseball here first and to Mexico and Venezuela, too.[12]

However, baseball as a manifestation of U.S. colonization cannot be ignored, inasmuch as "almost all the nations and territories producing Latin players today have been invaded by U.S. troops in the last century: the Dominican Republic, Cuba, Puerto Rico, Mexico, Panama, and Nicaragua. And if it wasn't an invasion by American troops, it was American business that organized the sport."[13] This neocolonial aspect of baseball is clearly expressed in the words of A. G. Spalding, the sport's premier entrepreneur and "missionary," who took a touring team across the globe in 1888–89: "Base Ball has 'followed the flag' . . . and wherever a ship floating the Stars and Stripes finds anchorage today, somewhere on a nearby shore the American National Game is in progress."[14]

U.S. eyes viewed the proliferation of baseball as part of manifest destiny, but assimilation appears not to have been the response generated by the encounter with Latin America. Like
globalization, colonialism reflects an intercultural encounter
that inevitably changes all sides of the power equation for better and for worse. "The local situation can seldom keep globalizing forces out altogether (and frequently does not want to),
and so it is inevitably changed by the encounter. . . . But local
situations are not powerless either. They work out all kinds of
arrangements, from syncretic borrowing to living in subaltern
systems."[15]

In Cuba the complexity of its relationship with the United
States, "the despised but intimate other," is reflected in its rejec-
tion of U.S. influence while simultaneously defining itself by
absorbing that influence.[16] According to scholar Roberto
González Echevarría, "Baseball, an American game, established
itself as the national sport of Cuba during an American occupation of the island because Cuban teams defeated American ones.
The conqueror's mantle of superiority in economic and military
power could not be denied, but it was removed in the mock
battlefield of sports."[17] This experience was not exclusive to
Cuba. Even though baseball was introduced to the Dominican
Republic by Cubans at the end of the nineteenth century, "it was
during the epoch of the North American occupation that baseball was really ignited. These games with North American sailors and marines were very important. There was a certain kind
of patriotic enthusiasm in beating them."[18]

Caribbean baseball distinguished itself from its U.S. counter-
part in the area of racial integration. In post Spanish-American-
War Cuba, for example, the professionalization of baseball challenged racial barriers. While much is justifiably made of the
integration of professional baseball in 1947 by Jackie Robinson,
ignored are the interracial teams composed of players from the
Caribbean, Negro, and U.S. major and minor leagues that played
winter ball together throughout the first half of the twentieth
century. Through this mezcla, "the game's national borders were

pierced by the players' itinerant style."[19] The attraction of Caribbean winter ball for U.S. professional players of all races was undoubtedly economic, motivated by financial remuneration in the off season. However, as early as 1908, in Havana, interracial baseball was more of a normative experience for U.S. players than U.S. baseball mythology cares to admit. "Once Americans left their native shores, they were able to shed racial prejudices long enough to risk baseball hegemony not only before the Cubans but also with their own black compatriots. . . . A space was being created where pleasure and sport displayed all their evil lures but where certain divisions and animosities could be put aside temporarily."[20]

There was a degree of reciprocity to this relationship. While there were Latinos who played on U.S. major league teams prior to Robinson's breaking of the color barrier, the history of the U.S. Negro Leagues is also replete with Spanish surnames and curious team names. The ambiguously named Cuban Giants, later called the Cuban X Giants, and the Latino-owned New York Cubans hint at lost stories of Hispanic participation on "both sides of baseball's racial fault line" and reveal "how the story of racial exclusion is much more textured than a mere black-white dichotomy would allow."[21]

Since the turn of the twentieth century, U.S. baseball has been described in mythic proportions wrapped in religious language and reflected on in theological terms.

> Caught up in liberal-Protestant currents of the turn-of-the-century Progressive Era, baseball epitomized both a faith in America's unique standing as a nation and the hope that the game could open a door leading to a better future. The kingdom of baseball contributed to the game's mythic stature by depicting the sport as a transcendent phenomenon that enabled Americans to clarify their nation's past, embrace a shared vision of the present, and affirm a common hope in the future.[22]

Baseball provided an opportunity for the development of moral and national character. It served as an outlet for "muscular Christianity," promoting a triumphant yet decidedly male, rugged piety, and modeled a democratic paradigm where "Americans from different class and ethnic backgrounds could work cooperatively to build a better society."[23] From F. Scott Fitzgerald's allusion to baseball as "the faith of fifty million" in *The Great Gatsby* to the "church of baseball" reference in the film *Bull Durham,* to Ken Burns's television documentary *Baseball,* religious language and imagery abound in popular U.S. cultural appropriation of the sport. Yet the overwhelmingly significant and storied Latino contribution is absent from virtually every mainstream popular and scholarly reflection on baseball. "It is a story with muddled chapters and missing pages, significant events lost through the years because, until now, they were primarily known only in Spanish."[24] The Latin@ connection is viewed primarily as a post-integration experience noteworthy for the growing presence of U.S. Hispanic and Latin American players, who constitute 27 percent of Major League Baseball's rosters.[25]

Examined through a postcolonial optic, baseball can be recognized as an instrument of U.S. colonization that is transformed by subalterns into a symbol of nationalism when the Caribbean encounters in Cuba, Puerto Rico, and the Dominican Republic are taken into account. From an ethical perspective, Major League Baseball is a globalizing transnational that needs to address matters of corporate social responsibility, for example, with respect to player recruitment practices in the Dominican Republic or the impact of its business decisions on the local economies dependent on Puerto Rican and Dominican leagues. Viewed through the lens of lo cotidiano, the U.S. national pastime is not just a game with no larger point or meaning. Some would claim that "there is no point to hitting a baseball . . . beyond the fact that it is intrinsically enjoyable, satisfying and beautiful. Work is not accomplished, mouths are not fed, the world is not improved."[26] Yet from a variety of Latin American perspectives, béisbol is "a passion shared

by the thousands of impoverished boys who stake their lives on
a deeper more poignant version of the American dream where
baseball is their only hope."[27] Seen through ojos latinos, the
Danny Almonte episode is an example of disconnected discourse,
interpreted in the United States through the lens of a flawed and
narrow narrative with no appreciation for transnational Dominican lived experience within a global context.


## VIEWS FROM THE LUXURY BOXES
## VS. LIFE IN THE BLEACHERS

The furor in the United States that surrounded Almonte's age
discrepancy reflects a pervasive and uncritical acceptance of
baseball's national mythology and a failure to comprehend the
implications of the sport's global presence and influence on daily
lived experience. This was repeatedly evident in the language of
the discourse framed by U.S. experience presumed normative,
and in the ethical evaluation of the alleged offending behavior
and the subsequent assignment of blame.

The focus of many of the charges of unethical behavior was
Danny's father, Felipe de Jésus Almonte. The charges leveled
against him demonstrated an all-too-common tunnel vision that
presumes one's own context is normative. For example, the growing concern in the United States regarding the negative role of
adults in youth athletic programs caused some commentators to
view Almonte's situation as further proof of obsessive parental
involvement:

> What a piece of work Felipe Almonte must be. He moved
> his son to the United States, falsified birth documents and
> kept him out of school just so that he could dominate 12-
> year-old Little Leaguers on the diamond. Instead of raising
> his son, he took advantage of him and turned him into a
> little cheat. He, and any other adults who knew Danny's

true age, are pathetic, the worst stereotype of the Little League parent sprung to life.[28]

Other commentators chided Felipe Almonte for selfishly prioritizing potential financial gain over the long-term value of an education:

The thoughtlessness of a parent . . . has left a child without innocence and, worse, without an education. In his efforts to cultivate a player who would someday—preferably someday soon—command a salary of millions . . . Felipe Almonte neglected to enroll his son in school for the entire 18 months they both have lived in this country. According to his father, Danny has done nothing but "eat and play ball" since he arrived in America. Did it never occur to Almonte that his son might not achieve his father's nearly unattainable dream of becoming a successful career ball player?[29]

Viewed from a privileged perspective, it seems easy to impose dominant cultural values on others simply because they enter the United States, but self-righteous sanctimony neither feeds a family nor secures its future. Attributing selfish motivations to Almonte's parents and finding his father's greatest fault to be his failure to enroll Danny in school reveals how out of touch U.S. sensibilities are with respect to the conditions of one of its poorest neighbors in the hemisphere. Furthermore, it portrays either ignorance or indifference to the role major league baseball has played in creating the environment that fosters the limited options that shape daily lived experience in the Dominican Republic. Did it ever occur to this journalist that financial success is a relative concept? Danny Almonte had only to attract the attention of a MLB-sponsored Dominican baseball academy to make more money playing baseball as a teenager than most make in a year. Alan M. Klein explains:

Even Dominican players who fail to reach the major leagues
and play instead in American minor league cities are considered financially successful, and those who remain in the
baseball academies for two years and do not play in North
America at all still earn more money than they would in a
decade on the streets or in the cane field. . . . The young
man who signs with an academy will receive a bonus and a
first-year salary that together are roughly seven times his
father's annual income.[30]

Major League Baseball is a transnational entity. Béisbol is an
industry in the Dominican Republic, and the academies are the
outposts of U.S. market colonialism, "the physical embodiment
overseas of the parent franchise . . . it finds raw materials (tal-
ented athletes), refines them (trains the athletes), and ships abroad
finished products (baseball players)."[31] The presence of MLB in
the Dominican Republic has precious little to do with altruism
and everything to do with business and the availability of a cheap
labor force, "because the island creates players born with the
perfect combination of qualities desired by the major league
scout—baseball knowhow and a sense of desperation born in
poverty horrific even by Latin American standards."[32] It is a story
"of capitalism and cutthroat competition. It is a story in which
opportunity is held out like a lottery ticket that most impoverished Latin kids will never cash in."[33]

In the Dominican Republic, education is often sacrificed on
the altar of baseball to improve the lot of entire families and
even communities. Compare the experiences of major league
players, U.S.-born Dominican American Alex Rodriguez with
Dominican-born and raised Miguel Tejada. For Tejada, a former
shoeshine boy and garment factory worker from the barrio of
*los Barrancones,* making it through school was not a reality.

No one from his barrio had ever finished school. . . . He
didn't have college offers to use as leverage against his

meager bonus, or agents who could protect his interests, or parents who could help him maneuver the land mines of modern-day major league sports. He was just a kid with precious few English skills and no other compelling options in his life but to play baseball.[34]

Alex Rodriguez, on the other hand, the number-one draft pick in 1993, and the highest paid baseball player in the major leagues, was the top prep player in the United States. He was able to negotiate a generous contract from the Seattle Mariners by threatening to attend the University of Miami if his conditions were not met. Rodriguez comments on the role his place of birth undoubtedly played in his fortune. Instead of educational options and guaranteed millions, had he been born in the Dominican Republic, like his immigrant parents, "I'm sure I would have been a top prospect but maybe I would have gotten $5,000, or $10,000. Or maybe $4,000. . . . The point is, it would have been a much tougher road."[35] The difference between contexts is striking, and their implications for the future are jarring. "If an American athlete—no matter how disadvantaged—fails in his quest to become a highly-paid professional, that athlete is still an American and has a far greater chance at making a decent living than a Dominican. Failure for him means becoming an undocumented immigrant in the United States or returning to a place like *Los Barrancones*."[36] Even the hoop dreamers in the inner cities of the United States are theoretically guaranteed an education through high school and possibly beyond, insofar as the ticket to the National Basketball Association is punched through college basketball.

In the United States the Danny Almonte situation was portrayed as a scandal. Even the usage of the phrase "say it ain't so" in conjunction with commentaries on the incident raises the specter of the Black Sox scandal and the fixing of the 1919 World Series. The phrase, initially framed as the question of a kid to one of the alleged game-fixing players, "Shoeless" Joe Jackson, is a piece of imaginative journalism that some would suggest is fabricated propaganda that has perpetuated the scapegoating of Jackson.[37] This allusion recalls to the popular imagination the Black Sox scandal, and thus intentionally establishes a connection between Almonte and a memorable event when dishonesty sullied the alleged purity of the sport. The words of Kenesaw Mountain Landis, Major League Baseball's first commissioner, reflect the challenge posed to the grand narrative that supposedly shook baseball out of its innocence: "Baseball is something more than a game to an American boy. It is his training field for life work. Destroy his faith in its squareness and honesty and you have destroyed something more; you have planted suspicion of all things in his heart."[38]

These sentiments return in the rhetoric that surrounded Danny Almonte. The purity and moral simplicity once ascribed to professional baseball came under scrutiny in a postmodern age exposed to millionaire owners and players, though the irony of the sport's traditional relationships with gambling, unsightly spitting, alcohol, and tobacco (both in sponsorship and in the notorious behavior of players, including some with iconic status) does not often make it to the sports page. The myth shifts focus and the Little League becomes a New Age morality play. Here too the disconnect between the privileged view from the U.S. luxury boxes and the daily lived experiences of those in the global bleacher seats is underscored.

> Age scams plague Little League competition in the Caribbean region, particularly in Venezuela, the Dominican Republic and Cuba, where it feeds into the local industry of developing major league players for the U.S. market. But in America, the land of opportunity, perhaps no institution tries to speak more eloquently of getting a chance than Little League Baseball. Girls and boys who won't be good enough for high school ball, never mind the pros, have their turn at bat and also the opportunity to build friendships, learn teamwork, grow.[39]

Losing teams do not make it to the Little League World Series, and not all teams are created with equal access to fields, finances, uniforms, and equipment. Opportunities for youth to build teamwork and grow do not draw a television audience with higher ratings than some pro events. Little League is a business, and corporate sponsors follow the money. It is probably worth noting that the quality of the equipment and field used by the Bronx team only improved as it became known for its winning and determined ways.

The preoccupation in the United States with the perceived lying aspect of the Almonte situation further highlights the hypocrisy of the national pastime. The opening of spring training 2002 brought a flurry of activity regarding visa problems and age corrections. As a matter of illustration, the following Dominican players were among the more than fifty in the major and minor leagues who aged post-Almonte: Rafael Furcal of the Braves; Timo Perez of the Mets; Ruben Francisco of the Orioles; Ramon Ortiz of the Angels; Bartolo Colon of the Indians; Delvi Cruz of the Padres; Neifi Perez of the Royals; Ed Rogers of the Orioles.[40] Why are these cases not regarded as "another sad saga of an overreaching parent undermining a cherished institution and abusing the trust of others."[41]

What if these cases—like Almonte's—demonstrate a pattern of response to the systemic injustices associated with the Dominican Republic's long and complicated relationship with the United States and baseball? What happens when we consider the possible reasons behind age deception practiced by Dominicans? While a different standard of record keeping and reporting account for some discrepancies, the consequences of poverty—for example, the impact of malnutrition on physical development—account for a need to level the playing field. A couple of years really do matter in the pursuit of the American dream, as the release of Marcus Agramonte by the Texas Rangers proves. He was an appealing prospect at nineteen, but when it was discovered that he was twenty-five, he suddenly became marginal.[42] For many of the Dominican aspiring athletes béisbol is about work, putting food in many mouths, and improving their local piece of the world. This interrelationship is captured in the expression that "embodies their competition against Americans for the precious spots on big league rosters: *Quitándoles la comida.*"[43] This expression, literally translated as "taking away their food," reveals that for some, baseball truly is about the basics necessary to survive.

Deception concerning age, when interpreted through the lens of daily lived experiences of Dominican youth and their families, may well be responses of accommodation and resistance. Parallels can be drawn with Brian Blount's discussions of African American slaves and the moral distinction they made between stealing and taking: "It was wrong to 'steal' something from another slave; it was, however, not only appropriate but also moral to 'take' from an owner. . . . The underpinning came from their understanding of a God who could not tolerate the indignity of their oppression and who approved of whatever actions were necessary to survive it."[44]

Blount cites the testimony of former slave Henry Bibb as an example: "I hold that a slave has a moral right to eat and drink and wear all that he needs, and that it would be a sin on his part to suffer and starve in a country where there is plenty to eat and wear within his reach. I consider that I had a just right to what I took, because it was the labor of my hands."[45] Blount goes on to point out that the ultimate form of taking from the master was escape, whereby the slaves raised "their own ethical ante" and each flight contributed to "a growing civil disobedience against the slave system" that each individual owner supported.[46]

A view from the bleachers suggests that perhaps the Dominican masking of age raises the "ethical ante" in a manner compatible with racial masquerading as practiced by Latinos and African Americans in U.S. baseball in the late nineteenth century and the first half of the twentieth century. Spanish-speaking peoples (especially from the Caribbean) complicated the U.S. construction of race. "Members of the Caribbean world who would have otherwise been considered non-white, if not black, gained certified admissions to compete in the major leagues by using the power of cultural and racial markers to reconfigure social rules."[47] The racial ambiguity of these Caribbean players subsumed under more "white friendly" ethnic labels as Latin or Castilian allowed them to cross over the racial divide in U.S. organized baseball. However, the nominal whiteness that this identification imparted did not change their marginal status confirmed by their use of the Spanish language. "Latino participation in racial masquerade in North American baseball is more complex and varied than the shorthand word *passing* would denote."[48] On the other hand, the use of Spanish was employed by some African Americans to acquire the more racially ambiguous labeling associated with their Spanish-speaking Caribbean counterparts. Two examples are worth citing.[49] African American Albertus Fennar, who was recruited in 1934 and played with the Havana Cuban Stars, received the Spanish pseudonym Roger Dario Fennar and learned some basic Spanish from his Cuban recruiters to complete the masquerade. The creation of the all–African American Cuban Giants in 1885 also suggests creative manipulation of racial categories. While there is debate over the veracity of the claim that the players spoke gibberish to each other in an attempt to appear Cuban, the fact that they assumed a Cuban moniker remains intriguing. Adrián Burgos suggests that convincing others of the authenticity of the players' identity is not the important element here: "Rather, the coy manipulation of the possibility of being Cuban made the masquerade successful and posed the most significant challenge to U.S. racial categories by inserting consideration of nationality and ethnicity."[50]

## BACK TO THE TABLE: INSIGHTS AND ETIQUETTE

As Latina and Latino theologians reflecting from within our varied U.S. contexts, how do we remain ethically responsible in our engagement among ourselves and with others? What informs

our table etiquette? Whom do we invite to our tables? Who comes
to our banquets? Whose tables are we invited to as guests or
even as familia?

Orlando Espín reminds us that any theology of grace is dependent on the daily lived experience of the theologian and his
or her local community.[51] In other words, our first ethical responsibility is to acknowledge and recognize that each of our
own respective culturally specific vidas cotidianas influence our
individual methodologies, foundations, and starting points for
reflection. Theologies that emerge from U.S. Hispanic perspectives bear an integrity marked by an openness to admitting that
our voices are situated. I reflect on béisbol not as a disengaged
scholar or as a devoted fan. Growing up in the Bronx, I had two
career paths in mind that did not appear impossible or mutually
exclusive: catcher for the New York Yankees and archbishop of
New York. I was raised on baseball, and my dad taught us to
play. My tía worked for the Yankees, and to this day their games
can be heard in the background at family gatherings. Summer
afternoons and birthdays were often spent at Yankee Stadium,
occasionally at Shea, or tossing a Spalding in front of the house.
When Jesus failed to deliver, I intervened with the Virgin on only
one matter: a baseball glove. Like many of the kids in the Dominican Republic, I too fashioned a glove from cardboard, in
my case six-pack soda cartons, and played catch with a found
golf ball in these homemade contraptions to simulate hard ball.
The praying finally paid off on my twelfth birthday, courtesy of
my father. The gender line was finally breached in Little League,
but it was too late for me. No manicured fields of dreams for
ball-playing girls in the Bronx; we made do with softball on black-
top schoolyards. I have become a fan of Puerto Rican winter
league ball in recent years and count among my treasures numerous baseball cards, an old wool Yankee cap, that very first
glove, and one Wilson baseball from Hiram Bithorn Stadium
(home of the Santurce Cangrejeros), clearly marked *Liga de
béisbol profesional de Puerto Rico*. My concern for Danny
Almonte arises in part from a shared youthful dream and from a

very intentional preferential option for the young on my part. Doing theology responsibly means honestly accepting the fact that a theologian's experiencia cotidiana has a significant impact on the way theology is done, for theology is never a disembodied enterprise.

Theologies emerging from Latin@ perspectives have been in the lead in elevating the popular—that which is from and of the people—as legitimate sources of theological reflection, as loci for the critique of systemic injustices, and as a means of hope, fostering survival often in the midst of dehumanizing conditions. We must take care not to limit the purview of what is considered popular and worthy of reflection to overt expressions of religious devotion. As the example of béisbol demonstrates, we cannot afford a complacency that permits religious language and theological reflection in this area to remain restricted to the articulations of males operating from exclusively dominant cultural U.S. contexts. Béisbol was, is and remains a significant part of pan-Latin@ identity and of resistance to victimization across the Americas. "Consequently, whether as fans or as players, participation in baseball cultivated a sense of pride and commonality and helped assuage the toll of physical relocation, economic exploitation, and racialization in U.S. society."[52]

If we are to be ethically responsible in doing theology, we must remain open to other revelatory expressions within our own daily lived experiences and those of the communities to whom we are accountable. At the same time, that openness cannot be naive or uncritical. Popular expressions also participate in sinful structures, as the interconnectedness of baseball and béisbol demonstrate. Globalization does not just happen to people; it is integrated within our daily lived experiences, and in turn those experiences with their needs and wants feed the global marketplace. The fluidity between local and global, globalizing forces and daily lived expectations, cannot be overestimated. For example, the colonizing impact of Major League Baseball in the Dominican Republic goes under-challenged precisely because there appears to be little benefit in biting the hand that feeds. If poverty is the catalyst, then exploitation is its byproduct. Baseball dreams are first nurtured in the home. Academies, while sponsored by MLB, are dependent on local Dominican baseball experts and entrepreneurs. Professional baseball salaries feed the local economy. Sammy Sosa is both the source of hurricane relief efforts and the sponsor of his own baseball academy. A young boy is publicly criticized for his sin of age deception while jokes are made on televised MLB broadcasts about the number of cakes a recently outed professional Dominican player should receive on his birthday. A number of high profile and very rich Dominican players are prominently featured throughout the major leagues, but who cares about what happens to the 90–95 percent of all foreign-born players signed to professional contracts who are cut before making it in the Grandes Ligas? Where is the outrage from la comunidad?

By its very nature the metaphor of table implies exclusion. Tables can accommodate only so many guests. At the same time, tables create conditions for a depth of engagement not possible in other modalities. As theologians it is necessary for us to gather in and around a table that enables a level of sustained engagement, and as Latin@ theologians we cannot delude ourselves into thinking this table is entirely inclusive, for it is not. That is not necessarily negative; inclusion for the sake of inclusion is not a value. "Inclusion touches upon the deepest human yearnings for belonging. But if inclusion means a complete erasure of difference, does it still remain an ideal?"[53]

If our doing of theology is to remain ethically responsible, than we must be respectful of the varied perspectives and lived experiences each of us brings to the table. We must be open to inclusion; open to invitations to other tables, particularly those that stretch our comfort zones; and we must be hospitable to those we invite to our tables, especially when it is most difficult and uncomfortable. We must also be honest and realistic: comprehensive inclusion is never possible; the truly inclusive table is an eschatological hope.

The ethical questions we grapple with as theologians concern what we are to do now and how we are to live in this in-between time, especially

> in those situations where our gender, race, class, national-
> ity, or other factor has placed us in positions of power, or
> where we have been invited as "tokens" to tables set by
> others. Banquet tables (ostensibly for fun and the celebra-
> tion of our success and acceptance) become for us work
> tables where we learn a method of resistant reading [*and I
> would add living*] that breaks through the "trained inca-
> pacity" that is the product of our ambivalent status as colo-
> nized and colonizers at the same time.[54]

How are we to live? Perhaps like the kids in barrios across the Caribbean who "pick up a stick, dig their toes into the scalding dirt, and stand ready for their pitch. . . . With hope and resolve, and with all their hearts, they swing as hard as they can."[55]

# 8

# Beyond Hospitality

## Implications of (Im)migration
## for Teología y Pastoral de Conjunto

I am at the stage in my life where most of us would crave stability, yet I find myself as part of the global phenomenon of "people on the move." I come from the Bronx; I live in Washington; I work in Chicago; and in the "off-season" I teach across the country for a couple of weeks here and there to supplement my income. As a professor in a Catholic graduate school of theology and ministry I am a gray-collar theological migrant worker. I use the term *gray collar* to refer to those among us in professions like teaching who augment salaries during semester breaks, sometimes with labor traditionally understood as blue collar. If you ask me where home is I will tell you New York, though I have not lived there in decades, but that is where my family lives. In the past few years the words of bi-national, bilingual poet Francisco Alarcón have taken on a special and quite literal significance for me: "mis raíces las cargo siempre conmigo enrolladas me sirven de almohada. I carry my roots with me all the time/ Rolled up I use them as my pillow."[1]

I concur with Fernando Segovia's honesty about the situatedness of our theologies, reflected in his admission that his life story is foundational for his scholarship.[2] In my migrations I do

110

not experience the dangers and injustices lived by refugees and those among us who lack the proper documents. This is thanks to decisions made by grandparents on both sides of my family who made their journeys to ensure that their children would be born and/or raised in the United States. Nevertheless, my family story is not very different from so many in this latest wave of migrations to North America. My Slavic father's oldest brother came as a toddler and earned his citizenship by serving in the U.S. Army and surviving World War II. My uncle's experience is not unlike a number of the more than thirty thousand foreign nationals in the U.S. military today, who dream of becoming citizens through their service. My mother's parents detoured through Cuba from Spain, victims of a revised immigration system. They married and conceived their firstborn in Cuba, and like so many today, their migration to the United States bears unexplained contradictions in documentation. From their journeys my inheritance includes a fondness for plátanos; an inexplicable level of comfort in the Spanish-speaking Caribbean; knowledge that a guagua is a bus, not an exotic lizard; and the responsibility to wear a white shirt as a sign of solidarity to a commitment that transcends generations.[3] Migrations are not objects of disengaged study but rather sources of theological reflection that emerge from mi vida cotidiana. Moreover, as a Hispanic theologian, rooted in an appreciation of teología y pastoral de conjunto, I see no demarcation among theological disciplines that sets pastoral theology and practical concerns as separate and secondary fields of study in the church and the academy.

One of the advantages of doing theology latinamente is that our recognition of lo cotidiano as locus theologicus allows us to accept the reality that all theology is local.[4] Therefore, to reflect on migration abstractly, removed from the context of real people and communities in complex situations, is counterintuitive and unproductive. Our local theologies arise from our communities of accountability, and these communities are multidimensional. In the context of migration to, from, and through the United

States, Puerto Rico, Mexico, and Canada, our communities and
churches include migrants and their families, border patrol agents
and federal judges, politicians and policymakers of all stripes,
the conflicted and the xenophobic, the fearful and the threatened, minutemen and activists, companions and those struggling
to live as good neighbors. With this complexity of our communities in mind, I focus on four challenges for theological reflection and praxis latinamente: first, retrieving the lost memories
of las luchas from past migrations; second, cultivating dynamic
solidarity across difference; third, changing the language and
rhetoric that surrounds (im)migration; and fourth, avoiding the
temptation to spiritualize border crossings.

## RETRIEVING OUR STORIES

Author Alfredo Véa, in his novel *The Silver Cloud Cafe*,
poignantly dedicated to migrants, challenges the cultural amnesia that plagues the United States:

> You must seek out remembrance, for ours is a land of am-
> nesiacs who pretend that there is no past; that America is a
> multi-cultural land when, in truth, it is an anticultural place
> that has ever been blessed with persistent and enduring
> cultures that have survived never-ending efforts to drag them
> out of sight; push them out of mind; to imprison them in
> the past.[5]

Later in the book Véa unmasks the price paid for such forgetful-
ness: "Americans run away from their old names, their old dia-
lects, from extended families, from relationships. They run from
languages, from people of color. The aggression of racism and
the hatred against the *bakla* are more ways of running."[6]

All theology is local! "This is America. When Ordering, Speak
English," proclaims the laminated sign in South Philly's Geno's

Steaks, proudly placed there by the owner, Joey Vento, the grand-son of Italian immigrants.[7] Vento's conviction, grounded in a flawed understanding of his own country's immigration policies prior to 1921, is not the exception in our churches and commu-nities. Indeed, our ecclesial institutions may well have contrib-uted over the years to an assimilation and white-washing of count-less (im)migrants to the point where the sacrifices and struggles of ancestors emigrating from other lands have been sanitized, romanticized, and idealized. This leaves their descendants with-out the context necessary to be in solidarity with or even toler-ate the presence of those who come seeking the very same things that their ancestors sought. How as theologians, ministers, and communities of faith do we heal cultural amnesia? How do we provide the tools, resources, space, and support necessary for our communities to begin the risky prospect of retrieving their own—our own—stories?

## DRAGGING THE MIDDLE TO THE EDGE

All theology is local! At the end of June 2006 in the Catholic Diocese of Tulsa, Oklahoma, a pastoral visit by Bishop Edward Slattery uncovered "a sense of disruption," articulated by a num-ber of the founding English-speaking members of a parish up-set with the active outreach initiated by a relatively new pas-tor.[8] The bishop himself came under fire for celebrating confirmation predominantly in Spanish. As the meeting became more heated, Slattery was shocked to hear a parishioner de-clare, "Yes, and I'll drive a bus," in response to whether or not all those without acceptable documentation should be deported. "You have something to learn here," the bishop replied, "and it's the gospel."[9]

Beneath the layers of fear was not only ignorance about the church's social justice teachings but an experience of displace-ment on the part of some in the Anglophone community. The disconnect between the church's teachings and the lived experience of this particular community is mirrored across the Catholic continuum in North America. The inability of church leadership to communicate this profound tradition of social justice in a concrete manner that makes sense to the grassroots remains an obstacle to the task of justice. For over a century the Catholic Church has developed and proclaimed a dynamic tradition grounded in respect for the fundamental dignity of all human beings and ensured by defense of basic human rights, including the right to migrate. Yet this tradition sadly remains unknown to many of the faithful. This ignorance leads to the conclusion expressed by one frustrated parishioner to Bishop Slattery: "The Catholic Church should have a plan."[10]

For our churches to have any impact beyond the immediate signs of our tiempos mixtos[11] we must move and sometimes drag the center to the edge and the edge to the heart of the center.[12] Lest we forget, the middle that requires some dragging also includes nuestra comunidad latina. The reality of our community's growing affluence, influence, and value as a market is a source of pride and tension. La lucha, for increasing numbers of our people—ourselves included, considering the privileged position of scholars—entails aspiration to and maintenance of a comfortable material existence. However, the focus of Hispanic ministry in many of our churches attends necessarily to the needs of the least of our hermanas y hermanos. This is not always well received. The proceedings of a national symposium of Catholic Hispanic ministries reports:

> This focus has led, at times, to tensions between new immigrants and U.S.-born Hispanics. The recent influx of new immigrants from Mexico and Central America into areas traditionally populated by Puerto Ricans, Cubans, or Mexican Americans is presenting new challenges to Hispanic ministry in dioceses throughout the country. Adding to this complexity are other ethnic groups with comparatively small

migrations, such as Latinos of African descent who have
long suffered racial prejudice, as well as indigenous peoples
from rural regions of Mexico and other countries who may
possess a low level of Spanish literacy.[13]

Those of us who have struggled to arrive in the economic
middle can also be threatened, and solidarity can be an impedi-
ment to our social mobility. Even so, there are signs of hope. A
survey by the Center for the Study of Latino Religion shows that
"74 percent of Latinos want their churches or religious organizations to aid undocumented immigrants even when providing
such help is illegal."[14]

## CHANGING THE RHETORIC

There is a disturbing trend in immigration rhetoric, as exem-
plified by news commentator Lou Dobbs, to refer to those who
migrate in dehumanizing terms. No matter one's position on
immigration reform, there is a need to examine critically the
public language used to refer to people on the move, especially
with respect to those who settle in communities and nations without the necessary documentation. The ongoing public rants that
play on the fears and insecurities of citizens unjustly categorize
(im)migrants at best as burdens on society and at worst as potential terrorists. Labeling human beings illegals and/or aliens
desensitizes individuals and communities to our shared humanity, grounded in our creation in the divine image. Humans are
not illegal, actions are; migration is a human right with responsibilities, not a criminal act. Furthermore, the association of migrants and immigrants as disease bearers, especially in this age
terrified of pandemics, harkens back to Nazi rhetoric about Jews
and others deemed detrimental to the state.
For Mexicans who came to the United States in the first half
of the twentieth century as immigrants and/or day laborers, the

humiliation of being disinfected at the border was all too real. What began as an attempt to prevent typhus remained U.S. Public Health Services policy for decades, a response disproportionate to the threat of possible outbreak. Those who crossed the southern border were required to endure delousing inspections that subjected them to being stripped, medically examined, bathed in kerosene or gasoline solutions, and later, for guest workers in the Bracero Program of the 1940s and 1950s, fumigated with DDT. The disparity of policy between the U.S. northern and southern borders ensured that "the pathologization of Mexicans represented an extension of the association of immigrants with disease into new racial and metaphorical terrain.[15] The cost of collective dehumanization has been paid many times over in human suffering, and the stains remain on the churches, communities, and nations who remained passive in the presence of injustice.

But language can create distance even when used by those with the best of intentions. There is a need for theologians, ministers, educators, and scholars to examine critically our own use of language in our scholarship, teaching, preaching, and ecclesial statements. For example, there is a tendency to use the third person when referring to people on the move. *We* are church and *they* are the stranger. We make an option for them.

This carelessness with language is also evident in ecclesial documents that reflect on diversity. Too often diversity is synonymous with difference, and difference means the immigrant, the minority, or the under-represented plurality. Diversity is a constitutive condition of our humanity, our globe, our nations, our churches. Diversity is not a characteristic of some who are in our midst; it is who we *all* are. The words of Chicano author Luis Alberto Urrea express this far more poetically. In *Nobody's Son* he writes: "My life is isn't so different from yours. My life is utterly alien compared to yours. You and I have nothing to say to each other. You and I share the same story. I am the Other. I am you."[16]

## SPIRITUALIZING OUR DISCOMFORT

There is a temptation for some of us involved in ministry and theology to spiritualize those experiences that make us profoundly uncomfortable. While certainly the quest for freedom of religious expression has prompted population movements across the centuries, more often than not migrations have been motivated by the need to eat, to feed one's family, to survive conscription and violence, to secure a future that might not be possible at home. There are certainly those who migrate out of adventure or occupation. Yet, for many, movement also implies loss; there are physical, psychological, economic, relational, and social implications. To impose spiritual interpretations on las vidas cotidianas of those who constitute our communities of accountability is exploitative, manipulative, and to a degree voyeuristic. To romanticize migration and canonize those among us who migrate is to dehumanize and disregard the particularity of each life.

Naive interpretations of border crossings as resurrection experiences downplay the ongoing uncertainty and risk of life in the "promised land." All theology is local, but as the divisive anti-immigrant legislation in Hazelton, Pennsylvania, gained national momentum, we were reminded of how easy it is for the promise to dissolve. Neighbors turn in neighbors, families are separated even in detention, and job security takes on new meaning as raids threaten the daily rhythm of work. These are concrete human lives, not object lessons to deepen our faith or opportunities to exercise the corporal acts of mercy.

Exaggerated spiritualization conceals the more complex role religion certainly has to play. Sociologist Manuel Vásquez observes:

Religion helps immigrants imagine their homelands in diaspora and inscribe their memories and worldviews into the physical landscape and built environment. In addition, religion regenerates and re-centers selves challenged by the migration process, producing new habituses, introducing new forms of collective and individual identity, and new understandings of citizenship, loyalty and community. Although these processes are 'imagined,' they are not inconsequential; they have tangible effects on space, time, and the body.[17]

As proposed legislation, policies, and practices aimed at migrating peoples across Canada, the United States, and Mexico have become increasingly harsh and family unfriendly, the prophetic role of our churches as sanctuaries and advocates will continue to be tested. There may indeed come a moment like that experienced by our hermanos y hermanas in Puerto Rico not too long ago over the U.S. Navy's use of Vieques as a bombing range. Rev. Heriberto Martínez, then secretary general of the Council of Churches of Puerto Rico, framed this prophetic challenge:

> In addition to individual spiritual issues, the church had to denounce sin and announce hope. Vieques shook us from a colonial mentality which kept the religious domain apart from the social. It made us realize that we can't just say the Our Father, while remaining silent in the face of injustice. When the highest leaders of the churches decided to take part in civil disobedience, the church had to confront its role in society.[18]

In his Ash Wednesday sermon on March 1, 2006, Cardinal Roger Mahoney, the archbishop of Los Angeles, called for civil disobedience on the part of the church's ministers should anti-immigrant bill HR 4437 become law. This controversial stance urging civil disobedience if confronted with injustice was not new. Catholics would do well to remember that the Diocese of Caguas, Puerto Rico, with the leadership of its bishop, Alvaro

Corrada del Río, "established a peace camp in February 2001, trained people to do civil disobedience, and produced user-friendly resources to help members understand the Vieques issue."[19] Among the ecumenical group of 180 people arrested on May 4, 2000 for civil disobedience were Bishop Corrada del Río, whose diocese included Vieques, as well as "34 nuns, 18 priests, 7 seminarians, and many deacons and lay people."[20]

The contemporary contexts of (im)migration challenge Latin@ scholars, ministers, and theologians to comprehend teología y pastoral de conjunto as a prophetic invitation to retrieve lost memories, to cultivate solidarity, to humanize our discourse, and to respect the integrity of immigrants' own stories. Hospitality is not enough. Even the posture of hospitality contains a hidden power differential revealed in the sentiment of a parishioner from that Tulsa, Oklahoma, parish: "The English-speaking parishioners have tried to be welcoming to the Hispanics. But many feel the newcomers have not reciprocated and that the Anglos' contributions are not valued."[21] The power resides on the side of the one who has the ability to choose to welcome or to turn away. The problem with hospitality as the predominant paradigm is that current usage of the language of "stranger" fails to appreciate that the stranger is not only the newcomer to the land, but also the inhabitant encountered by the sojourner.

# 9

# Justice Crosses the Border

## The Preferential Option
## for the Poor in the United States

Since Medellin in particular, the Church, clearly aware of its mission and loyally open to dialogue, has been scrutinizing the signs of the times and is generously disposed to evangelize in order to contribute to the construction of a new society that is more fraternal and just; such a society is a crying need of our peoples. Thus the mutual forces of tradition and progress, which once seemed to be antagonistic in Latin America, are now joining each other and seeking a new, distinctive synthesis that will bring together the possibilities of the future and the energies derived from our common roots. And so, within this vast process of renewal that is inaugurating a new epoch in Latin America, and amid the challenges of recent times, we pastors are taking up the age-old episcopal tradition of Latin America and preparing ourselves to carry the Gospel's message of salvation hopefully and bravely to all human beings, but to the poorest and most forgotten by way of preference.

—THIRD GENERAL CONFERENCE
OF THE LATIN AMERICAN EPISCOPATE, PUEBLA[1]

Arising from the heart of the Latin American experience, the expression "preferential option for the poor" appeared in 1979 at Puebla de Los Angeles, México, in the final document of the Third General Conference of the Latin American Episcopate.[2] More than a year later it was repeatedly affirmed by Pope John Paul II during his 1980 visit to Brazil. In his July 10 address to the Brazilian bishops, he explained:

> You know that the preferential option for the poor was strongly proclaimed at Puebla. It is not a call to exclusiveness, it is not a justification for the bishop to omit to announce the word of conversion and salvation to one or another group of persons on the pretext that they are not poor. After all, what is the context that we do give this term? . . . It is a call to special oneness with the small and weak, those that suffer and weep, those that are humiliated and left on the margin of life and society.[3]

In its journey across the Americas, the notion of the preferential option as articulated at Puebla faced and continues to face the problems associated with border crossings—detainment and misunderstanding—as well as the challenges of creating a new life in a new place and transforming the place of encounter. In the contact with the United States the question raised echoes the question of John Paul II on Brazil: "After all, what is the context that we do give this term?"

Within the context of U.S. Hispanic theologies, the principle of the preferential option for the poor is appropriated as a foundational characteristic of theologies of liberation. In the words of María Pilar Aquino, we "must reaffirm that the option for the poor and oppressed does not belong to a past theological paradigm; rather, it remains a fundamental Christian imperative—a required norm for the protection of our rationality."[4] It is precisely this significance that invites a closer examination of the mediation and appropriation of this principle within the United States. Therefore, this chapter traces the use of the expression through representative pastoral statements by U.S. bishops, individually and collectively. This will make it possible to gauge a context for ascertaining the current level of understanding, communication, reception, and appropriation of the preferential option for the poor within the Roman Catholic Church in the United States. If this principle is to transform the place of encounter and in turn be transformed by its appropriation in this new place, then it is crucial to the ongoing conversation to track its journey.

A survey of the signs of the times suggests the urgency with which the preferential options for the poor—and the young—must be revisited and re-imagined within the context of the United States, in particular from the perspectives of Latin@ theologians, whose reflections tend to privilege lo cotidiano, everyday experience. Statistics provide a window into the complexities that constitute the daily reality of U.S. Hispanic experiences. Theologians need to contend with these glimpses, as they often prove to be signs of contradiction.

The Census Bureau reports that for Latin@s the poverty rate increased in 2007 to 21.5 percent, up from 20.6 percent in 2006.[5] At the same time, Hispanic purchasing power closes in on one trillion dollars. With a discretionary income that exceeds the gross domestic product of Mexico, Michael Barrera, CEO of the U.S. Hispanic Chamber of Commerce, tells CNN that Latin@s constitute "the second largest economy in North America."[6]

As the United States moved into the twenty-first century, the digital divide was described as a "racial ravine" where the information rich outpaced the information poor with cyber speed. Having access to computers and to the Internet was considered key to successful social integration, but the reality at the time was that a digital divide negatively affected those most in need of technology as a resource.[7] Discrepancies in access, abetted by the cost factor, were estimated to take a toll on minorities and female-headed households where members used the Internet to conduct job searches and pursue online courses in order to improve their current status. Now, according to a 2008 report by the consumer and media research firm Scarborough Research, 54 percent of Hispanics are online. "Hispanic Internet access has grown 13% (on a relative basis) since 2004. . . . By contrast, Internet access by all consumers nationally grew 8% during the same time period. In 2004, 64% of all consumers accessed the Internet, and this increased to 69% in 2008."[8] However, the study also determined that half of Hispanic Internet users had a household income exceeding fifty thousand dollars a year.[9] This is something worth noting, because the "median income for Hispanic households was $38,679 in 2007, which was 70 percent of the median for non-Hispanic White households."[10] A posted reader response to an optimistic column using the Scarborough study to challenge the "digital divide" underscores the inherently complicated and even contradictory interpretations of the economic state of la vida latina. According to one comment:

> There is a real digital divide in this Nation and although the so-called expert research indicates advancement by Hispanics, the reality in Main Street USA is that a very large number of Hispanics don't have access nor use the Internet on a daily basis, unless using your digital Metro PCS phone with unlimited calling to the US and Mexico is considered "surfing the Internet."[11]

Theologians can ill afford to ignore the reality that for increasing numbers of U.S. Hispanics, liberation involves upward mobility and an SUV. As Hispanics rapidly move into the vast middle, the experience of Jeff Valdez, creator of the cable television family "The Garcia Brothers," is both enlightening and alarming. The show was test marketed using two different types of Latin@ families: recent immigrants struggling to make it versus an assimilated suburban middle-class family. Hispanic focus groups "vociferously voted against the downscale family. They asked, 'Why do we have to always be poor and drive lousy cars and speak in accents?'"[12] The painful legacy of poverty and abiding stereotypes calls for structural answers and contextual reflection—crucial elements of the transformative praxis of Latin@ theology.

## ACROSS THE BORDER: THE U.S. CONTEXT

Prior to the September 1984 "Instruction on Certain Aspects of the 'Theology of Liberation'" by the Congregation for the Doctrine of the Faith (CDF), references to a preferential option for the poor appear in the pastoral letters and addresses of the bishops of the United States sporadically, primarily from those bishops who were either themselves from under-represented racial and ethnic minority communities or whose ministries were involved with these communities.[13]

One of the earliest references occurs in an address to the Catholic Press Association in May 1980 by African American Bishop James Lyke, O.F.M., then an auxiliary bishop of Cleveland and a member of the Committee for the Campaign on Human Development (CHD). Regarding the experience of the Catholic Church in Latin America and its predilection for the poor as a learning opportunity for the Catholic Church in the United States, Lyke presents the efforts of the CHD as an example of a "preferential, though not exclusive, love of the poor." He cites the criteria for CHD-funded programs as evidence of this determination. The majority of people served must fall below the poverty line, the projects must be controlled by the poor, and "projects should encourage various racial and ethnic groups, as well as the poor and not so poor to work together for justice."[14]

From Lyke's perspective, "CHD is a case where the church listens to the poor and is evangelized by them. The campaign does not dictate the methods to be used. . . . CHD receives applications from poverty groups which have themselves designed their own methods of addressing the causes of their poverty and oppression."[15] Furthermore, CHD funding supports self-help projects that seek to foster structural change by attacking the causes of poverty or by affecting the legal, policy, and decision-making processes that maintain poverty.

Essential to the preferential option for the poor, according to Lyke, is the need to empower the poor, to bring about structural and systemic change, and to appreciate the poor as an evangelizing force. From his perspective, the poor evangelize the church by opening eyes to injustices, sinful structures, and oppressive systems; by communicating a sense of urgency; by inviting a greater fidelity to the gospel; by calling for reexamination of lifestyles, especially in terms of consumption; by raising minds and hearts to the social dimensions of the Christian message. The poor "tell us that we are not saved as individuals but as a people and that all doctrine is social doctrine."[16] While remaining optimistic, Lyke recognized that "many of us perhaps feel that it would be a mistake to let the poor evangelize the church, because this would drag the church down. On the contrary, the church would be renewed if we let ourselves be evangelized."[17]

The application of a notion of preferential option for the poor to specific concerns and populations is evident in two statements affecting Hispanics that appeared between 1981 and 1983. Reflecting on 1981 as the fiftieth anniversary of Pius XI's social encyclical *Quadragesimo Anno* and the 450th anniversary of the appearance of Our Lady of Guadalupe, the bishops of the Santa Fe Province explored three themes that they attribute to Pope Pius XI, themes with particular relevance for their region as the "site of the confluence of three major ethnic cultures—Anglo, Mexican and Native American."[18] One of these themes, the church's preferential option for the poor, is identified as a "reoccurring papal concern about material poverty," with roots in scripture and the church's history. For these bishops, to be poor "is to die of hunger, to be illiterate, to be exploited and not know that you are being exploited. To be poor in this context is to be without choices. To be rich and powerful in terms of papal literature is to have a variety of alternatives and options from which a person may choose a course of action."[19]

The bishops insisted that the church's predilection for persons who are poor or oppressed does not imply the canonization of a particular social class, nor does it offer an assurance of "blanket salvation for the poor and condemnation for the rich."[20] However, they maintained that the option as a response to the sinful human condition of poverty carries social and religious consequences: "Persons with choices and therefore with power can do something to ameliorate the human condition for those in need and thereby contribute to the human development of the impoverished. . . . Persons with choices meet the Lord in a special way in the poor and their positive response to them can be personally redemptive, a 'measure' . . . of conscience, a way to the kingdom."[21] This interpretation is illustrated in the encounter between the Virgin Mary and the bishop mediated by Juan Diego, "a lowly Aztec Indian who had no stature in the new society of the Spaniards and who could not even speak Spanish, the language of the bishop."[22] Viewed through the lens of the Tepeyac experience, "the powerful are given the option to respond to God's intention through the presence of the poor."[23]

In the pastoral letter *The Hispanic Presence: Challenge and Commitment*, approved by the U.S. bishops at their 1983 national meeting, the expression appears in a context that appears to identify Hispanics with the poor. "We call all U.S. Catholics to work not just for Hispanics but with them, in order to secure their empowerment in our democracy and the political participation which is their right and duty. In this way we deepen our preferential option for the poor which, according to Jesus' example and the church's tradition, must always be a hallmark of our apostolate (Puebla, 1134)."[24]

The year 1984 emerged as a turning point in terms of the exposure the option for the poor receives in the statements of the U.S. bishops. In early September the CDF released its "Instruction on Certain Aspects of the 'Theology of Liberation.'" The congregation was quick to explain that this warning should not be interpreted as "a disavowal of all those who want to respond generously and with an authentic evangelical spirit to the 'preferential option for the poor.' . . . It is, on the contrary, dictated by the certitude that the serious ideological deviations which it points out tend inevitably to betray the cause of the poor."[25] Concerned by interpretations of the option for the poor that "transform the fight for the rights of the poor into a class fight within the ideological perspective of the class struggle,"[26] the CDF also affirms the positive meaning associated with preference given to the poor "without exclusion, whatever the form of their poverty, because they are preferred by God."[27]

In 1984 the option for the poor was very much on the minds of the U.S. bishops, with the November release of the first draft of their pastoral letter on the U.S. economy. The influence of the preferential option for the poor is evident in the three priorities guiding its direction: the basic needs of the poor should be fulfilled; increased participation by the marginalized takes precedence over the preservation of privileged concentrations of power, wealth, and income; and investment should be targeted toward meeting human needs and increasing participation.[28]

> First it imposes a prophetic mandate to speak for those who have no one to speak for them, to be a defender of the defenseless. . . . It also demands a compassionate vision which enables the church to see things from the side of the poor, to assess lifestyle as well as social institutions and policies in terms of their impact on the poor. Finally and most radically, it calls for an emptying of self, both individually and corporately, that allows the church to experience the power of God in the midst of poverty and powerlessness.[29]

Throughout the draft, the preferential option for the poor serves as a frame of reference for shaping the approach toward domestic and international economic issues.

The year 1984 concluded with a strong affirmation of the church's commitment to the preferential option for the poor by Pope John Paul II in his address to the College of Cardinals and in his Christmas message, *Urbi et Orbi*. Acknowledging the emphasis placed on the option by the Latin American bishops and reiterating his own commitment to the poor as a dominant motive of his pastoral action, John Paul II affirmed: "I have made and I do make that 'option' my own; I identify with it." He defended the "Instruction on Certain Aspects of the 'Theology of Liberation'" from distorted interpretations by contending that the document "constitutes an authoritative confirmation of it and effects a clarification and deepening of it at the same time."[30]

After two additional drafts (one in 1985 and another in April 1986), the U.S. bishops' pastoral letter on the U.S. economy, *Economic Justice for All*,[31] was approved in November 1986. In this pastoral the preferential option for the poor is affirmed as a "fundamental criterion for making moral judgments about economic policy."[32] It was understood by the bishops as a moral priority that obliges all members of society to "assess lifestyles, policies, and social institutions in terms of their impact on the poor. This 'option for the poor' does not mean pitting one group against another, but rather, strengthening the whole community by assisting those who are most vulnerable. . . . We are called to respond to the needs of *all* our brothers and sisters, but those with greatest needs require the greatest response."[33]

This meant recognizing as urgent objective: the fulfillment of the basic needs of the poor, a priority that precedes "the fulfillment of desires for luxury consumer goods, for profits not conducive to the common good, and for unnecessary military hardware;"[34] increased active participation in economic life by those currently excluded or vulnerable; investment of wealth, talent, and energy in efforts benefitting the poor or economically insecure; the evaluation of social and economic policies and the organization of the work world in light of their impact on the stability and integrity of family life.[35]

The attention paid to the poor did not go without notice, even in the earliest stages of the drafting process. As Cardinal Joseph Bernardin, archbishop of Chicago, noted: "The letter makes space in the policy debate for the fate of the poor in a way which has not been evident for some years now. We need to make space for the faces of the poor in our personal consciences and in the public agenda because the facts tell us that poverty is not so marginal in this nation as we might think."[36]

There were noticeable changes from the first draft to the final version in the treatment of the preferential option for the poor. *Economic Justice for All* credits the agency of the poor by asserting that decisions can be judged not only in terms of what they do *for* and *to* the poor but by "what they enable the poor to do *for themselves.*"[37] Later they state that the poor are not exempted from the obligations of solidarity and justice. "The guaranteeing of basic justice for all is not an optional expression of largesse but an inescapable duty of the whole of society."[38]

In November 1996 the U.S. bishops approved a one-page anniversary statement, "A Catholic Framework for Economic Life," outlining ten principles drawn from Catholic teaching on the economy. Third on the list was that "a fundamental moral measure of any economy is how the poor and vulnerable are faring."[39] In his remarks introducing the framework to the bishops, Bishop William Skylstad, chair of the Committee on Domestic Policy, suggested that it "calls us to focus on moral principles, not the latest polls; on the needs of the weak, not the contributions of the strong; and the pursuit of the common good, not the narrow agendas of powerful economic interests. . . . We need to be very clear. Our defense of the poor, our pursuit of economic justice is fundamentally a work of faith."[40] Who are those whose lives and dignity are to be defended? Skylstad tells us:

This is about children of God with names and faces, with hopes and fears. This is about the women who are cleaning our hotel rooms this morning for the minimum wage. This is about immigrants who will bus our dishes this afternoon. This is about the people who knock on our rectory doors, rely on our food pantries and live in cardboard boxes under bridges. This is about children dying in Africa this morning. This is not about the president or the speaker of the House. It's about people who make our sneakers and haul our trash. It's about people in corporate America trying to resist short-term pressures for long-term contributions to the common good. It's about the 55-year-old executive who is downsized and the family farmer who can't make it anymore.[41]

He concludes by reminding his brother bishops that ten years after their pastoral on the economy, there was still work to do. He urges them to support and actively to utilize this latest tool in applying and sharing the economic teaching of the church in the United States.

## MAPPING THE TRENDS

Twenty years after the introduction of the preferential option for the poor into theological and pastoral vocabulary and thirteen years after the formalization of the principle in the consciousness of the U.S. bishops, there is striking evidence that its journey north has met with obstacles. The difficulty in appropriating the principle in the United States is evident in the bishops' 1998 document on the implementation of social teaching on all levels of Catholic education. Acknowledging that the church's social teaching must no longer be treated as tangential or optional, the bishops admit that many Catholics do not comprehend these teachings as essential to the faith. Recognizing the power of education as integral to the transmission of this social mission and message, the bishops are also aware that "in too many schools and classrooms these principles are often vaguely presented; these values are unclear; these lessons are unlearned."[42]

This challenge to understanding is in part due to the manner in which discourse about the preferential option for the poor has been framed, communicated, and understood. It can even be argued that the preferential option for the poor crossed into the United States via Alitalia with papal statements and curial pronouncements as primary vectors. Prior to 1984, attempts were made to credit the Catholic Church in Latin America for its instrumental role in articulating the principle. Yet the distancing of the concept of the preferential option for the poor from its Latin American roots also begins early in the U.S. formulations.

The first draft of the U.S. bishops' pastoral on the economy mentions the emergence of the expression at Puebla as significant to church thought. In an address at the Catholic University of America in Washington DC shortly after the release of that draft, Cardinal Bernardin acknowledges that the concept was "rooted in the Scriptures, developed with originality by the Catholic Church in Latin America and now becoming a guide for ministry in the universal Church under the leadership of John Paul II."[43] By the third draft the Puebla reference was relegated to a footnote citation that begins with the Congregation for the Doctrine of the Faith's 1986 "Instruction on Christian Freedom and Liberation,"[44] released barely two months before the appearance of the draft.

In the pastoral letter of the Santa Fe Province bishops the preferential option for the poor is attributed to Pius XI, tenuously connected to a phrase in *Quadragesimo Anno*. The phrase in question appeared in the context of a discussion of the responsibility of civil authority for the protection of the common good. The latter portion of a line from section 25 is quoted by the Santa Fe Province bishops to indicate the papal provenance of the option for the poor: "In protecting the rights of private individuals, chief consideration ought to be given to the weak and the poor."[45]

The Santa Fe Province bishops were also strongly influenced by John Paul II's desire to be voice of the voiceless:

For the chief spokesman of the universal church to assume the role of advocate for the poor is consistent with the Catholic doctrine that the pope is the vicar of Christ. To be his vicar is to present the cause of the poor to those who can make a difference. In a word to speak for those who

have no choices, to speak to those who do have choices
and who therefore can choose to respond or to refuse to
respond.[46]

The selective memory reflected in U.S. episcopal formulations
unfortunately replicates the very marginalization and voiceless-
ness they seek to remedy. In effect, the gradual muting of Latin
American voices and the mediation of the preferential option
for the poor through the offices of the pope and CDF have perpetuated relationships grounded in privilege and power rather
than justice. Is it the authority of the Vatican that lends credibility to the claims of the poor, or is it the agency and conditions of
the poor, vulnerable, powerless, and silenced?

The marginalization of the poor and vulnerable is further evident in the language used to communicate this moral imperative. The agency of the poor is diminished both by what is said
and how it is expressed. The impression often given is that the
poor exist to enlighten or evangelize or raise the consciousness
of the non-poor. Whether it is Bishop Lyke's claim that the church
would be renewed if we *allowed* "ourselves" to be evangelized
by the poor or the Santa Fe bishops' perspective that the powerful are given the option to respond to God through the presence
of the poor, the result, despite the best of intentions, objectifies
the poor. Those without power or privilege are relegated to the
realm of depersonalized others with whom an encounter is instrumental in bearing utilitarian, if not salvific, benefits for those
among the privileged and powerful who choose to respond.

Consistent references to the poor and vulnerable in the third
person further increase marginalization while diminishing agency.
The repeated use of third-person pronouns in speaking of the
poor and first-person pronouns when speaking of the church or
the United States sets up a dichotomous "us" and "them" that
undermines talk of solidarity. This stigmatizes the poor further
by implying their disconnectedness from the church and the nation. For example, in the 1983 pastoral on Hispanic ministry,
the U.S. bishops call "all U.S. Catholics to work not just for

Hispanics but with *them*, in order to secure *their* empowerment in *our* democracy," thus deepening "*our* preferential option for the poor."[47] Granted the increased appreciation for the concept of empowerment that enables U.S. bishops to move from initiatives that do for and do to the poor toward enabling the poor to do for themselves. This carelessness with language nonetheless is counterproductive in terms of creating a sense of community, let alone true empowerment. The degree of separation between privileged and powerless articulated by this use of language is not a matter of nitpicking or trivialization, for such discourse ensures that agency remains in the hands of those with the choices and options.

This difficulty with discourse underscores a fundamental inability to conceptualize the preferential option for the poor as a manifestation of solidarity. Much of the controversy surrounding the appropriation of the principle is generated by an inability to conceive of it as an option *for* community, not against community. This is evident in the insistent refrain of non-exclusivity that accompanies the mention of the preferential option for the poor. In the Puebla document the Latin American bishops grant this concern fleeting attention, choosing instead to keep the focus on the poor: "This option does not imply exclusion of anyone, but it does imply a preference for the poor and a drawing closer to them."[48] In the 1986 "Instruction on Christian Freedom and Liberation," the CDF cautions: "The special option for the poor, far from being a sign of particularism or sectarianism, manifests the universality of the church's being and mission. This option excludes no one."[49] In his 1991 social encyclical letter *Centesimus Annus*, John Paul II notes that the preferential option for the poor is "never exclusive or discriminatory toward other groups."[50] In their pastoral on the economy, the U.S. bishops write that the "option for the poor" is not "an adversarial slogan that pits one group or class against another. Rather it states that the deprivation and powerlessness of the poor wounds the whole community."[51] This refrain is echoed in the words of Bishop John Kinney to the people of the Diocese of

St. Cloud: "The option for the poor . . . is a helpful way of understanding how we should respond to anyone in need."[52]

The temptation to frame the principle in adversarial terms, especially in the context of the United States, comes as no surprise. *Preference* carries baggage. In a climate charged with discussion of the pros and cons of affirmative action, the term *preferential* implies, for some, partiality and special treatment. This implication is clear in economist Milton Friedman's critique of *Economic Justice for All*: "We want greater opportunities for everybody. It is a mistake to regard the so-called poor as a special class. Not only are the poor at any time human beings like the rest of us, but the poor at one time are not the same as the poor at other times, and the very concept of who are 'the poor' is a matter of perception, not of fact."[53]

Friedman downplays the hard reality of poverty by making poverty and the poor a matter of perception rather than fact. Who *are* the poor? In crossing the border from Puebla to the United States, the definition of *poor* expands exponentially. In the Puebla document poverty is perceived through the lens of material deprivation and denial of access to means of economic sustenance.[54] In the subsequent appropriation of the principle, the option for the poor is not limited to material poverty but expanded to incorporate cultural and spiritual poverty as well. In a 1983 address to priests in El Salvador, John Paul II notes that the ordained minister is "called to make a preferential option for the poor, but he cannot disregard the fact that there is a radical poverty wherever God is not alive in the hearts of the people who are slaves to power, to pleasure, to money, to violence. He must extend his mission to those poor too."[55]

In his 1984 Christmas message John Paul II renewed the church's commitment to the preferential option for the poor, identifying the countless multitudes of the modern poor. He affirmed solidarity with the victims of famine, drought, and hunger; with refugees; with the unemployed; with those experiencing solitude and abandonment through sickness, old age, or misfortune; with widows and orphans; with those martyred for preaching the gospel and living the social teaching; with the kidnapped; with families suffering from the moral upheaval unleashed by consumerism; with those struggling to escape drugs, violence, and criminal organizations. The pope went on to express solidarity with "victims of those other forms of poverty which strike at the spiritual and social values of the individual." In this grouping he included those deprived of the right to freedom of movement, personal security, and life; those excluded by virtue of discrimination based on race or nationality; those denied expression of thought or of profession and practice of faith; those excluded or imprisoned for dissenting legitimately from a regime's ideology; those subjected to psychological violence, violating the sanctity of the conscience.[56]

In the United States the option for the poor is frequently amended to include the vulnerable, a category harkening back to the scriptural concern for the poor as well as widows, orphans, and strangers in the land, groups of people whose conditions suggest dependence and powerlessness. This expanded understanding of the marginalized does not lessen the rhetoric of inclusion. This is certainly reflected in the statement of Rembert Weakland, O.S.B., archbishop of Milwaukee and head of the economic pastoral's drafting committee. When he presented the first draft at the 1984 national meeting, he said: "As one would expect from Catholic bishops, we have a special emphasis on the poor. . . . But neither our pastoral vision nor our policy perspective is limited to our concern for the poor. They also extend to the near poor and the not-so-near poor."[57]

It is this ongoing refrain repeatedly raised on behalf of the not-so-near poor and the near poor that betrays a profound obstacle in the comprehension and acceptance of this principle in the U.S. context. Since the option for the poor arose within a Latin American context marked by great disparity between the very rich and the very poor, the lacuna in U.S. discourse is located in the underdevelopment of an understanding and articulation of the role of those who find themselves in the vast middle. While there is no disputing the existence of a disparity in wealth, access, and resources between the very rich and the very poor, in the United States these represent extremes, with the majority of people falling economically somewhere between these two poles. The failure to account for that middle ground has prevented the development of a U.S. interpretation of the preferential option for the poor that invites embrace.

As Allan Figueroa Deck has noted: "Poverty in the United States is not the reality of the mainstream, but that of the minority (albeit growing in recent times). The norm for most North Americans as well as for the growing numbers of the United States Hispanics is the middle-class way of life."[58] Citing work done by sociologist Andrew Greeley, Deck continues that U.S. Hispanics tend not to relate psychologically to identifications of themselves as poor, even though all too many meet the statistical definition of poverty. This inability to recognize the middle ultimately undermines solidarity and is counterproductive to the transformational power and intent of the option for the poor and vulnerable.

The challenge missed is how to enable individuals to evaluate personal choices, attitudes, lifestyles, savings, investments, and consumption habits in such a way as to appreciate their impact on others, especially on their neighbors at the margins. How does personal conversion effect structural transformation? How is one led to recognize interdependence not in terms of "vague compassion or shallow distress" but as a "persevering determination to commit oneself to the common good . . . to the good of all and each individual because we are all really responsible for all"?[59] Unfortunately, in dealing with personal response the emphasis has been on a particularly anemic understanding of charity, not justice, thus fostering the sense of vague compassion that does not lend itself to just relationships rooted in interdependence, but to one-sided dependence. Attention has primarily been concentrated on conscientization of those with power and privilege and to a lesser degree on the empowerment of the poor and vulnerable.

In his remarks to the Special Assembly for America, Bishop Ricardo Ramirez of Las Cruces, New Mexico, exhorted the bishops to "maintain as a major concern the weakest among us and recognize this as part of the law of charity and not just a gesture of benevolence."[60] This repeated identification of the principle as a manifestation of a distorted notion of charity rather than justice rooted in solidarity reduces the transformative potential of the option for the poor.

Catholic social teachings appear amorphous on this matter, contributing to the confusion that strips the poor and marginalized of their agency and voice. In *Sollicitudo Rei Socialis*, John Paul II identified the "option or love of preference for the poor" as a "special form of primacy in the exercise of Christian charity."[61] Yet in *Centesimus Annus* the pope sends what seem to be conflicting messages. Early in the letter he writes:

> It will be necessary above all to abandon a mentality in which the poor—as individuals and as peoples—are considered a burden, as irksome intruders trying to consume what others have produced. The poor ask for the right to share in enjoying material goods and to make use of their capacity to work, thus creating a world that is more just and prosperous for all.[62]

The impression is that the poor are active participants in transforming the world, partners in solidarity asking for their just place at the table.

Later in the same encyclical the pope claims, "Justice will never be fully attained unless people see in the poor person, who is asking for help in order to survive, not an annoyance or a burden, but an opportunity for showing kindness and a chance for greater enrichment."[63] The force of the first statement is reduced by the blandness of the second, in which the poor are placed in a position of inequality as suppliants of charity, objects who provide others with an instrumental opportunity. Although the pope did go on to say that this aid should be drawn from substance and not surplus goods and that it required a change of lifestyles and consumption models to enable the marginalized to enter into the sphere of human and economic development, damage is done to the notion of preferential option as an expression of justice. In the U.S. context this encourages an interpretation of the option for the poor as a hybrid of charity and justice, whereby charity is evident in the contributions of time, money, and resources, whereas justice is effected by the enactment of socioeconomic change through public policies, institutions, and legislation. As Bishop Ramirez observes, "While U.S. Catholics are generous in their charitable contributions, they lack a 'social conscience' and fail to go beyond charity to work for justice."[64]

Further attenuating the transformative power of the preferential option for the poor is a failure to appreciate its intergenerational potential. The preferential option for young people seems to have been detained at the border, without an opportunity to pack for the journey. In the final Puebla document this option follows the option for the poor and is discussed in some detail.[65] Unfortunately, the inclusion of this option has been interpreted as "playing down to some degree the uniqueness of the phrase 'option for the poor' and in this way making it less threatening and more widely accepted."[66] What this disregards is the disproportionate presence of the young among the poorest and most vulnerable, and the implications of that fact for the future. Left unexplored are the possibilities for transformation that exist if an option is made for youth, and if in turn the young themselves make an option for life on the margins.

The lack of attention to the option for the young did not go unnoticed. In the 1984 "Instruction on Certain Aspects of the 'Theology of Liberation.'" the CDF noted: "We should recall that the preferential option described at Puebla is twofold: for the poor and for the young. It is significant that the option for the young has in general been passed over in silence."[67] The precarious condition of youth did receive priority attention at the III Encuentro in 1985. In the "Prophetic Pastoral Guidelines"—

preceded by a preferential option for the poor and marginalized, and numbered third among the sixty-eight articles affirmed at the gathering—is a "preferential option for Hispanic youth so that they will participate at all levels of pastoral ministry."[68] This commitment to the young is fueled both by a concern for the experience of marginalization that is often heightened by poverty and issues of cultural identity and by faith in the prophetic voice of youth. The pastoral dimensions of the commitment are articulated in greater depth in articles 30 through 38. Though the term *preferential option for the young* is not explicitly used, it appears to inspire the under-utilized 1991 U.S. bishops' pastoral "Putting Children and Families First: A Challenge for Our Church, Nation and World."[69]

The discussion of the preferential option for the poor in the Puebla document includes the young at the top of its list of the many faces of the poor. Insistence on a preferential option for the young by no means distracts from the uniqueness of the preferential option for the poor. On the contrary, each heightens the urgency of the other. At Puebla a preferential option for the poor and a preferential option for young people were discussed in the context of evangelization. Both the poor and the young "constitute the treasure and the hope of the church in Latin America, and so evangelization of them is a priority task." Recognition is given that such evangelization serves to benefit the young who are seeking "to construct a better world," and the continent benefits as this evangelization guarantees "the preservation of a vigorous faith."[70] The young, like the poor, emerge as both the evangelized and, in turn, the evangelizers.

Shoved to the margins of the discourses on the options for the poor and the young is the role of gender as a marginalizing factor. While it is assumed that women are included among the poor and young, occasional references note their unique situation. In the Puebla document this occurs in a footnote recognizing that the women who constitute the poor are "doubly oppressed and marginalized."[71] In the discussion of youth, "negative features of women's liberation and a certain *machismo*" are identified as the culprits "blocking the sound advancement of women as an indispensable factor in the construction of society."[72]

In the U.S. context, women are also addressed as an afterthought, with references focused on their role in relationship to the raising and care of children. One exception appears to be the U.S. bishops' 1988 "National Pastoral Plan for Hispanic Ministry," grounded in the working document and conclusions of III Encuentro. Within the context of the discussion of a "preferential missionary option for the poor and marginalized, the family, women, and youth,"[73] the reality of a triple discrimination endured by women is acknowledged:

- Social (machismo, sexual and emotional abuse, lack of self esteem, exploitation by the media);
- Economic (forced to work without proper emotional and technical preparation, exploited in regard to wages and kinds of work, bearing full responsibility for the family, lacking self-identity);
- Religious (her importance in the preservation of the faith is not taken into account; she is not involved in decision making yet bears the burden for pastoral ministry).[74]

While the well-intentioned objective is "to promote faith and effective participation in Church and societal structures on the part of these priority groups . . . so that they may be agents of their own destiny (self-determination) and capable of progressing and becoming organized,"[75] the plan offers a weak form of concrete address, avoiding further discussion of the ramifications of the previously identified multiple levels of discrimination. Action is limited to a call for regional meetings with a focus on ministries by women.[76]

In the conversation about the options, women are denied agency and voice; their experiences of poverty and youth are mediated by others. Ignored is the empowerment of women and girls, whether on the margins or in the vast middle, to embrace, live, and shape these options as their own. Latina theologians have not been silent. María Pilar Aquino writes, "The women's perspective gives a special place to one aspect of the option for the poor: it wants to reach the questions, historical and spiritual experiences, knowledge, memory, desires, and expectations of women, not only as part of this suffering world, but primarily *as women*."[77]

## REDRAWING THE MAP

Roberto Goizueta has noted that "when read in the context of contemporary U.S. society, the preferential option for the poor—as developed most systematically by Latin American theologians—is susceptible to misinterpretation."[78] It is clear that U.S. bishops' statements about the preferential option for the poor explicitly draw neither on the work of Latin American bishops and theologians nor on the work of Latin@ theologians. As my survey of pastoral statements reveals, the primary dialogue partner remains Rome. It is surprising to realize the absence of Latin@ theological voices in the episcopal formulations that articulate a national investment in this option.

At the very least, enlightened self-interest should dictate that it is high time for this theological voice to enter the conversations, if not shape its course and development on the national level. As Cardinal James Hickey suggested in 1984, the fashioning of "our own preferential option for the poor" remains a pressing challenge, taking into accounts the context of the United States with its unique spectrum of abundance as well as marginalization.[79] There is a need to bridge, in a balanced manner, the distance between the Latin American roots of the option for the poor and its formal articulations in the United States. This calls for a recognition that "Latin American references to the poor and a spirituality forged from the perspective of the popular masses and their legitimate struggles for revolutionary change can seem strangely out of place and somewhat off target

for the United States Hispanics."[80] At the same time, it calls for
reclaiming of the option for the poor as enunciated at Puebla to
counteract the trend of

> reversion to a more abstract, spiritualized understanding
> of the option for the poor. Solidarity with the poor, now
> defined as the culturally marginalized, can be effected sim-
> ply through "consciousness raising" rather than through a
> practical identification with the political and economic
> struggles of the poor.[81]

Investment in the transformative potential and lived experience of a preferential option for those on the margins requires
outreach to and engagement by those who populate the vast
middle ground as well as to and by the young. This is especially
urgent for Latin@s. Statistics reveal endemic marginalization
among Hispanics: a disproportionately large number live in poverty; the population is characterized demographically by its youth-
fulness; the school dropout rate is alarming; anti-immigrant re-
sentment and violence continue and even escalate; and
discrimination toward the public use of the Spanish language
finds protection in the law. On the other hand, the Hispanic
experience is also marked by an attraction to and increased presence in that vast middle described appropriately by one African
American writer as "someone who is one step out of poverty
and two paychecks from being broke. I have income but not
true wealth."[82] Frequently, in the particular case of the Latin@
immigrant, at least one of those checks is being sent to support
family in the nation of origin.

It is this ground, with its ambiguous promise of the American
dream, that writer Junot Díaz portrays in his short stories, a
social geography replete with moderate- to low-income apart-
ment complexes "surrounded by the malls, cineplexes and mu-
nicipal pools of the middle class."[83] Díaz comments on how often writers of color, like himself, are reared in suburban and
middle-class environments, yet portray low-income people in their

works: "It shows that even writers are responding to pre-set notions of who 'we' are and how 'we' are supposed to be viewed."[84]

From a Latin@ perspective the preferential option for those on the margins entails accompanying the poor, as well as bringing the middle to the edges that some would rather forget. In order to ensure that amnesia does not become a permanent condition, "you must simultaneously touch the center of society and move the center—sometimes *drag* the center to the margins, where the poor and powerless can be found."[85]

The encounter between Latin@s established in the United States and more recent immigrants reinforces the urgency with which this twofold responsibility must be assumed. One Latina, raised in the United States since the age of three, calls the widening cultural gap between newcomers and Latin@s who immigrated decades ago "willful distancing," observing that there exists "very little help from established Latinos to the newcomers. . . . There's little social conscience. But that is not necessarily unique to Latinos."[86]

Unfortunately, the "Americanization" of Hispanics with respect to the poor and marginalized is apparent in attitudes that perpetuate the "otherness" of recent immigrants and that frame poverty in terms of personal and moral failure. This is evident in the words of a highly accomplished fifty-one-year-old Salvadoran who became a U.S. citizen in 1970. In thirty years she has gone from being a dishwasher to one of the few Hispanic administrators in the District of Columbia public school system. "There's a big difference for us who came first," she tells the *Washington Post*. "It was harder to make it, yet we had the strong moral values. For us, the United States was *una casa ajena* (someone else's home), so we had to show the best of us even to those who thought we were invading. We had to show we had something to offer. But this generation is totally different."[87]

The gap and its correlative dichotomy between "us" and "them" are manifest in the admission by a successful son of Colombian immigrants who is a neighbor to newcomers from rural Central America: "They come for economic reasons or human rights reasons. . . . It's kind of alien to me because my family is fairly well off. . . . As far as exposure to these people, I haven't had that much. There's distance. My ties to the first generation aren't very strong at all."[88]

Hispanic theologians need also be cognizant of both the privileged (if not comfortable) position we occupy in the middle by virtue of our education and employment in addition to the marginalization we encounter in the academy, the society, and the churches because of the perspectives and experiences we attempt to bring to the table. It is from this unique social location that Latin@ theologians can view through bifocal lenses perspectives both from the margins and the middle ground to cultivate and model relationships born of the mutuality that solidarity presupposes.

> Solidarity helps us to see the "other"—whether a person, people or nation—not just as some kind of instrument . . . but as our "neighbor," a "helper" (cf. Gn. 2:18–20), to be made a sharer on a par with ourselves in the banquet of life to which all are equally invited by God.[89]

It is not to be a voice for the voiceless but to ensure that those silenced have access, especially in this advanced technological age, to the basics, resources, and structures to find and exercise their own voices.

In order to be transformative, the preferential option for the poor and vulernerable calls for practical engagement in daily, personal, and public life. However, the discourse regarding the option remains primarily on the abstract level with minimal description. This is illustrated by the 1998 bishops' pastoral "Sharing Catholic Social Teaching: Challenges and Directions." It would seem that a statement specifically targeting the need to integrate social teaching in all areas of Catholic education would take care to communicate in concrete and accessible language a heritage they admit is unknown by many Catholics. The document was informed by a task-force report that highlighted the reality that for too many Catholics in the United States, social teaching is not viewed as essential to the faith and that in educational settings the teaching is not sufficiently integral and explicit.[90] The task force drew on assessments from people in ministries across the nation that underscored the confusion surrounding the understanding of the preferential option for the poor. It is worth nothing that in the final task-force report the phrase "preferential option for the poor" was replaced by "compassion for the poor," and the specific concern regarding the understanding of the option is not referenced. The section on the preferential option for the poor that finally appeared in the U.S. bishops' education document is all too brief. Once again the option for the poor is articulated without pictures, a surprise considering the intended audience comprises educators charged with conveying the message to and engaging the creativity and commitment of the young. Lacking imagination, the passage merely reiterates what has come before.

When the bishops do use concrete examples, they tend to be limited, drawn mainly from the provision of social services, emergency interventions, and the enactment of political or legislative change. For example, Bishop Kinney's pastoral letter explains that the option for the poor means "we strengthen, not diminish, already existing programs such as food shelves, parish-sponsored meals for needy persons, shelters for the homeless. . . . It could mean legislation on wages to ensure that Bill and other workers do not work full time and still remain in poverty. It could also mean striving for changes in our health care system that will guarantee every person's right to basic medical treatment."[91]

Implicitly operative in this example is a characteristically hybrid interpretation of the preferential option for the poor found in U.S. formulations that appears to place charity in the sphere of the personal, and justice in the sphere of the public. This is underscored in the report of the content subgroup of the aforementioned task force on social teaching and Catholic education.

In its description of the option for the poor as a basic principle of Catholic social teaching, the subgroup understands the response to all, especially those with the greatest needs, as accomplished "through acts of charity, through meeting the immediate needs of those who are poor and vulnerable, as well as through our own participation in society, shaping political and economic institutions that meet basic needs, promote justice and ensure the participation of all."[92]

A lack of images and concrete examples hampers the communication, understanding, and integration of the preferential option for the marginalized in the U.S. Catholic lived experience and imagination. The church has failed to heed its own advice that those "who preach should always bear in mind that the ability to hear is linked to the hearer's language, culture, and real-life situation."[93]

## FINDING THE OPTION FOR THE POOR IN NUESTRAS VIDAS COTIDIANAS

The challenge to re-imagine and rearticulate the preferential option for the poor and vulnerable in a manner that invites engagement and commitment requires the discovery and recovery of windows that offer glimpses into how the option for those on the margins can be lived. Three examples illustrate the option lived in lo cotidiano.

In Dalton, Georgia, self-described carpet capital of the world, a major influx of Mexican and Central American immigrants was greeted with innovations designed "not only to ease the immigrants' transition to American life, but to create a new, more bilingual community."[94] Facing classrooms where the increased enrollment of Spanish-speaking students threatened to paralyze the school system, the community responded by seeking to make all students fluent in both English and Spanish. This entailed the establishment of a partnership with the University of Monterrey in northern Mexico, whereby graduates of that university were granted temporary work visas in order to staff schools with bilingual instructors, and U.S. teachers were sent to Monterrey for intensive language and culture classes.

The community as a whole has benefited from this option made for the most vulnerable, in this case the stranger in the new land. Immigrant workers have well-paid jobs to support their families; the town has improved economically; all the children of the town have the opportunity to be fully bilingual; second- and third-generation Hispanics living in Dalton have reclaimed their linguistic and cultural heritage; and a partnership grounded in a mutual exchange has developed between towns on opposite sides of the border. A main consideration in the design of the bilingual programs, known as the Georgia Project, was the intention to avoid "the regrettable yet frequent mistake made in numerous schools throughout the world: to place languages in competition, as if one were a more legitimate human communication vehicle."[95]

In 1993, in Alexandria, Virginia, a group of nurses opened a neighborhood health clinic in response to growing numbers of Hispanic schoolchildren without immunizations and of uninsured Latinas without prenatal care giving birth at home, all too often to babies with preventable birth defects. "'I don't see what we do as charity and I don't see the city's role as providing charity,' Executive Director Susan Abramson said. 'I do see our role as investing in a population that needs investment. To protect and promote its own welfare as a city, the city needs to help all its citizens be productive, healthy residents.'"[96]

In Washington DC a public-service advertisement sponsored by United Cerebral Palsy was posted in Metro stations throughout the region. The ad depicted the beneficial features of the transit system, including elevators, flashing lights signaling the approach of a train, announcements indicating impending stations, and a tone warning passengers about the opening and closing of car doors. The question posed in the ad, "Did you know people with disabilities make your commute easier?" was answered with the simple statement "Access for One Means Access for All."

Fashioning a contextualized preferential option for the marginalized in the United States needs articulation and illustration. This is a task Hispanic theologians are in a position to appreciate, considering the primacy accorded experience and location as valid loci for theological reflection in a contextual framework. This is a task that the work of Latina feminist theologians has prepared us to embrace by their emphasis on the daily lived reality of the Hispanic experience and by including a deliberate option for women in the preferential option for the poor.[97]

As theologians who share in the Latin@ experience in the United States understand, for many here the preferential option for the poor is a preferential option for family scattered across the Americas. This is a task that requires the imagination and openness to recognize the preferential option for the poor and vulnerable in the daily encounters of ordinary lives lived in solidarity.

## SOLIDARITY IN THE AGE OF BENEDICT XVI

The first social encyclical of the twenty-first century was published in July 2009, in the fifth year of Benedict XVI's pontificate. Originally scheduled for release in 2007 (to mark the fortieth anniversary of Paul VI's *Populorum Progressio*), the global financial crisis postponed the publication of *Veritas in Caritate*. As Benedict XVI notes, "The current crisis obliges us to re-plan our journey, to set ourselves new rules and to discover new forms of commitment, to build on positive experiences and to reject negative ones."[98] This delay underscored the dynamic intent of social teaching as engagement with the signs of a given and changing time.

This third encyclical from the pen of Benedict XVI met with mixed initial response. For example, George Weigel went so far as to propose a hermeneutic strategy that distinguished what he concluded were the words of Benedict, "a truly gentle soul," from those of the Pontifical Council for Justice and Peace. In his "cafeteria Catholic" parsing, Weigel suggested that readers mark in red the alleged influence of the Pontifical Council for Justice and Peace on matters that focused more on the "redistribution of wealth than about wealth-creation." A gold marker could then be used to highlight what Weigel judged to be Benedict's attention to his "trademark defense of the necessary conjunction of faith and reason and his extension of John Paul II's signature theme—that all social issues, including political and economic questions, are ultimately questions of the nature of the human person."[99] Curiously, Weigel dismisses papal initiative in this exercise and minimizes the more challenging aspects of the encyclical by referring to Benedict XVI as a "gentle soul." What appears to disturb Weigel most cannot simply be excised from this encyclical, that is, the thread of solidarity that holds the whole text together. In a tone of frustration, he writes:

> Some of these are simply incomprehensible, as when the encyclical states that defeating Third World poverty and underdevelopment requires a "necessary openness, in a world context, to forms of economic activity marked by quotas of gratuitousness and communion." This may mean something interesting; it may mean something naïve or dumb. But, on its face, it is virtually impossible to know *what* it means.[100]

Quite to the contrary, I assert that there is no ambiguity in this encyclical. For Benedict XVI, *caritas* is at the heart of social doctrine. "It gives real substance to the personal relationship with God and with neighbour; it is the principle not only of micro-relationships (with friends, with family members or within small groups) but also of macro-relationships (social, economic and political ones)."[101] At the same time, without truth, charity "would be more or less interchangeable with a pool of good sentiments, helpful for social cohesion, but of little relevance. ... It is excluded from the plans and processes of promoting human development of universal range, in dialogue between knowledge and praxis."[102] A relational perspective permeates the encyclical, and solidarity is an expression of mutually account-able relationships. The word *solidarity* appears over forty times in the text, excluding the notes. For Benedict XVI, subsidiarity must accompany solidarity, "since the former without the latter gives way to social privatism, while the latter without the former gives way to paternalist social assistance that is demeaning to those in need."[103]

What is strikingly absent, however, is any specific mention of the preferential option for the poor. John Paul II defined this principle of Catholic social teaching as a "special form of pri-macy in the exercise of Christian charity" in both *Sollicitudo Rei Socialis* and *Centesimus Annus*.[104] However, Benedict XVI's attempt to rehabilitate charity from misuse avoids the principle altogether. He acknowledges:

> Charity has been and continues to be misconstrued and emptied of meaning, with the consequent risk of being mis-interpreted, detached from ethical living and, in any event, undervalued. In the social, juridical, cultural, political and economic fields—the contexts, in other words, that are most exposed to this danger—it is easily dismissed as irrelevant for interpreting and giving direction to moral responsibil-ity.[105]

For Benedict XVI, "Charity always manifests God's love in human relationships as well, it gives theological and salvific value to all commitment for justice in the world."[106] Charity presumes justice, and these two inseparable companions are not alterna-tive or even parallel paths. In Benedict XVI's schema, and con-trary to many popular U.S. understandings, the agency of the poorer partner, whether individual, community, or nation, is not reduced to supplicant status. Drawing on his papal predecessors,

Benedict XVI understands that those among us who are poor are not a passive burden; they are, rather, both valuable resources and active participants in the process of development. This is evident in the encyclical's critique of development efforts, whereby "those who receive aid become subordinate to the aid-givers, and the poor serve to perpetuate expensive bureaucracies which consume an excessively high percentage of funds intended for development."[107] Charity, with its interwoven expectation of justice, requires a solidarity manifest in "the active mobilization of all the subjects of civil society, both juridical and physical persons."[108] Whether or not this explication of *caritas* can rehabilitate perceptions of charity in the U.S. context remains to be seen. As demonstrated earlier in this chapter, the benevolent generosity of charity in popular practice and imagination is often not connected to perceptions of or actions on behalf of justice.

While *Caritas in Veritate* does not specifically mention the option for the poor, that concern is implicit throughout the encyclical's call for a solidarity of presence and praxis that is inclusive. *Caritas in Veritate* analyzes the contemporary global situation from the perspective of the impact of policies and practices on the lives of the most vulnerable. At the same time, those most in need are not treated as objects but as partners sharing a responsibility for ensuring the common good, as "a requirement of justice and charity."[109]

> Every Christian is called to practise this charity, in a manner corresponding to his vocation and according to the degree of influence he wields in the *polis*. This is the institutional path—we might also call it the political path—of charity, no less excellent and effective than the kind of charity which encounters the neighbour directly, outside the institutional mediation of the *polis*.[110]

In this way Benedict XVI reaffirms the option for the poor without specifically naming it. However, the absence of this principle by name raises some concern, especially in light of its difficult crossing into U.S. Catholic imaginaries. The prophetic insistence of the jarring expression *preferential option for the poor* constituted a standing invitation to reflect critically, analyze, educate, and act. It was a call to shared responsibility, a solidarity that demanded more than shallow compassion. Without it, "while the poor of the world continue knocking on the doors of the rich, the world of affluence runs the risk of no longer hearing those knocks, on account of a conscience that can no longer distinguish what is human."[111]

# Notes

## Introduction

1. Fernando F. Segovia, "The Text as Other: Towards an Hispanic American Hermeneutic," in *Text and Experience: Towards a Cultural Exegesis of the Bible*, ed. Daniel Smith-Christopher (Sheffield, UK: Sheffield Academic Press, 1995), 285.

2. José R. Irizarry, "Lost in Translation: The Challenges and Possibilities of Ecumenical Dialogue," *New Theology Review* 21, no. 4 (November 2008): 43.

3. Juan Flores, *From Bomba to Hip-Hop: Puerto Rican Culture and Latino Identity* (New York: Columbia University Press, 2000), 158.

4. Ibid.

5. For a detailed compilation of this rich theological heritage, see Gary Macy, "The Iberian Heritage of Latino/a Theology," in *Futuring Our Past: Explorations in the Theology of Tradition*, ed. Orlando O. Espín and Gary Macy, 43–82 (Maryknoll, NY: Orbis Books, 2006).

6. To learn more about ACHTUS, see http://achtus.org/ and the *Journal of Hispanic/Latino Theology* at http://www.latinotheology.org.

7. I borrow the expression "dissident cartographies" from a multimedia project commissioned by the Sociedad Estatal para la Acción Cultural Exterior (SEACEX) of the Spanish government. The project includes a book, *Dissident Cartographies,* José Miguel G. Cortés, curator (Barcelona: SEACEX, 2008).

## 1. We Are Not Your Diversity, We Are the Church!

1. Martín Espada, "Sheep Haiku," in *Alabanza: New and Selected Poems 1982–2002* (New York: W. W. Norton, 2003), 210.

2. Luis N. Rivera-Pagán, "A Prophetic Challenge to the Church: The Last Word of Bartolomé de las Casas." Inaugural lecture as Henry Winters Luce Professor in Ecumenics and Mission, April 9, 2003, Princeton Theological Seminary.

3. Orlando Espín, "An Exploration into a Theology of Grace and Sin," in *From the Heart of Our People: Latino/a Explorations in Catholic Systematic Theology*, ed. Orlando Espín and Miguel Díaz (Maryknoll, NY: Orbis Books, 1996), 126.

4. Ada María Isasi-Díaz, *Mujerista Theology: A Theology for the Twenty-first Century* (Maryknoll, NY: Orbis Books, 1996), 71.

5. Miguel Díaz, *On Being Human: U.S. Hispanic and Rahnerian Perspectives* (Maryknoll, NY: Orbis Books, 2001), 115.

6. Department of Communications, United States Conference of Catholic Bishops (USCCB), "Catholic Information Project: The Catholic Church in America—Meeting Real Needs in Your Neighborhood" (May 2005), 4. Available on the usccb.org website.

7. Ibid.

8. Ibid., 5.

9. Secretariat for Hispanic Affairs, USCCB, "Hispanic Ministry at a Glance." Available on the usccb.org website.

10. "Number of Hispanics Entering Ministry Continues to Grow," USCCB Media Blog (April 2, 2009).

11. Mary L. Gautier, "Catholic Ministry Formation Enrollments: Statistical Overview for 2005–2006" (Washington DC: Center for Applied Research in the Apostolate, Georgetown University, April 2006), 11.

12. Ibid., 30.

13. Mark M. Gray and Mary L. Gautier, "Summary of 'Latino/a Catholic Leaders in the United States,'" in *Strengthening Hispanic Ministry Across Denominations: A Call To Action*, ed. Edwin I. Hernández, Milagros Peña, Rev. Kenneth Davis, CSC, and Elizabeth Station, Pulpit and Pew Research Reports (Durham, NC: Duke University Divinity School, 2005), 19.

14. USCCB, "Encuentro and Mission: A Renewed Pastoral Framework for Hispanic Ministry," Appendix, no. 75.

15. ATS, "Diversity in Theological Education" Folio (PDF), see "Racial/Ethnic Enrollment by Decade, 1969–1999" (table) and "Full-Time Racial/Ethnic Faculty in ATS Member Schools 1980, 1991, 2001" (table). Available on the ats.edu website.

16. ATS, *2008–2009 Annual Data Tables*, "Table 2.18 Head Count Completions by Degree Program, Race or Ethnic Group, and Gender, All Member Schools." Available on the ats.edu website.

17. Established in 1996 with a grant from the Pew Charitable Trusts, the Hispanic Theological Initiative took up as its mission the creation and nurturing of "a community of Latina/o scholars to service the academy and the church. Its primary goal is to increase the number of Latina/o students and faculty in theological education and, by doing so, better equip US institutions to serve the growing Hispanic population" (Hispanic Theological Initiative, History; available on the www2.ptsem.edu website).

18. Caroline Sotello Viernes Turner et al., "An Evaluation: Perspectives on the Hispanic Theological Initiative," *Perspectivas* (Fall 2005): 65.

19. Cardinal Francis George, quoted in Manya A. Brachear and Margaret Ramirez, "Catholic School Closings: Latino, Black Parishes Hit Hardest by Decision," *Chicago Tribune* (February 25, 2005).

20. Richard Szczepanowski, "Archdiocese Issues Hispanic Pastoral Plan, 'Diverse in Culture, United in Faith,'" *Catholic Standard* (June 8, 2006).

21. Rev. Raúl Gómez and Dr. Manuel Vásquez, "Hispanic Ministry Study." Available on the usccb.org website.

22. USCCB, Hispanic Affairs Committee, "Encuentro 2000." Available on the usccb.org website.

23. Ibid.

24. USCCB, "Encuentro and Mission," no. 8.

25. Ibid.

26. USCCB, "Encuentro 2000."

27. USCCB, "Encuentro and Mission," n.2.

28. Fernando F. Segovia, "Theological Education and Scholarship as Struggle: The Life of Racial/Ethnic Minorities in the Profession," *Journal of Hispanic/Latino Theology* 2, no. 2 (1997): 14n19.

29. "U.S. Bishops' Proposed Reorg Plan Drastically Reduces Committees," *Catholic News Service* (June 1, 2006).

30. Bishop Gerald F. Kicanas, "Monday Memo," 4, no. 12 (June 19, 2006). Available on the website diocesetucson.org.

31. USCCB, "Encuentro and Mission," Appendix, no. 69.

32. Ibid.

33. Justo L. González, "Reading from My Bicultural Place: Acts 6:1–7," in *Reading from This Place: Social Location and Biblical*

*Interpretation in the United States,* ed. Fernando F. Segovia and Mary Ann Tolbert (Minneapolis: Fortress Press, 1995), 146.

34. María Pilar Aquino, "Theological Method in U.S. Latino/a Theology," in Espín and Díaz, *From the Heart of Our People,* 36.

35. Fernando Segovia, "Two Places and No Place on Which to Stand: Mixture and Otherness in Hispanic American Theology," in *Mestizo Christianity: Theology from the Latino Perspective,* ed. Arturo J. Bañuelas (Maryknoll, NY: Orbis Books, 1995), 35.

36. Juan Flores, *From Bomba to Hip Hop: Puerto Rican Culture and Latino Identity* (New York: Columbia University Press, 2000), 8.

37. Roberto Goizueta, *Caminemos con Jesús: Toward a Hispanic/ Latino Theology of Accompaniment* (Maryknoll, NY: Orbis Books, 1995), 163.

38. Ibid.

39. Segovia, "Theological Education and Scholarship as Struggle," 14n19.

40. James Nickoloff, "The Word Entombed," paper presented in the Latino/a Theology group at the Sixtieth Annual Convention of the Catholic Theological Society of America, 8. See Gary Riebe-Estrella, "Latino/a Theology," *Proceedings of the Sixtieth Annual Convention of the Catholic Theological Society of America* 60 (2005), 142–43.

41. Nickoloff, "The Word Entombed," 5.

42. Ibid., 9.

43. Min Seo Park was ordained to the (transitional) diaconate in July 2006 in the Archdiocese of Seoul, South Korea. On July 6, 2007, he was ordained a priest.

44. Goizueta, *Caminemos con Jesús,* 147–48.

45. Ed Morales, *Living in Spanglish: The Search for Latino Identity in America* (New York: St. Martin's Griffin, 2002), 29.

46. Samuel P. Huntington, "The Hispanic Challenge," *Foreign Policy* (March/April 2004): 45.

47. Aquino, "Theological Method in U.S. Latino/a Theology," 37.

48. Ada María Isasi-Díaz, "A New Mestizaje/Mulatez: Reconceptualizing Difference," in *A Dream Unfinished: Theological Reflections on America from the Margins,* ed. Eleazar Fernandez and Fernando Segovia (Maryknoll, NY: Orbis Books, 2001), 219.

49. Jean-Pierre Ruiz, "Good Fences and Good Neighbors? Biblical Scholars and Theologians," *Journal of Hispanic/Latino Theology* (May 27, 2007); available at latinotheology.org. Also see Andrew Irvine,

"*Mestizaje* and the Problem of Authority," *Journal of Hispanic/Latino Theology* 8, no. 1 (August 2000): 5–37; and Nestor Medina, *Mestizaje: Remapping Race, Culture, and Faith in Latina/o Catholicism* (Maryknoll, NY: Orbis Books, 2009).

50. See, for example, Jacques Audinet, *The Human Face of Globalization: From Multicultural to Mestizaje* (Lanham, MD: Rowman and Littlefield, 2004); and Zipporah Glass, "The Language of *Mestizaje* in a Renewed Rhetoric of Black Theology," *Journal of Hispanic/Latino Theology* 7, no. 2 (November 1999): 32–42.

51. Morales, *Living in Spanglish*, 29.

52. Ibid., 31.

53. Darrell H. Y. Lum, "Local Genealogy: What School You Went?" in *Growing Up Local: An Anthology of Poetry and Prose from Hawai'i*, ed. Eric Chock, James R. Harstad, Darrell H. Y. Lum, and Bill Teter (Honolulu: Bamboo Ridge Press, 1998), 11.

54. Ibid., 12.

55. Stephen H. Sumida, *And the View from the Shore* (Seattle: University of Washington Press, 1991), xvii, as cited in Lum, "Local Genealogy," 11.

## 2. Decolonizing Practical and Pastoral Theologies

1. For example, Latin@ contributions are absent from an otherwise valuable publication, *Pastoral Care and Counseling: Redefining the Paradigms*, ed. Nancy J. Ramsay (Nashville, TN: Abingdon Press, 2004). See pages 71, 140, and 145 for mentions in passing.

2. Some Latin@s do identify in this way. For example, Allan Figueroa Deck, S.J., writes, "As a practical theologian, I began to look at the unfolding Latino/a drama several years ago. . . . I used a simple pastoral-theological tool, the "see-judge-act" method also called the pastoral circle" (Allan Figueroa Deck, "A Latino Practical Theology: Mapping the Road Ahead," *Theological Studies* 65 [2004]: 276–77).

3. Jean-Pierre Ruiz, "U.S. Hispanic/Latino Theology: The 'Boom' and Beyond." Formerly available at www.shc.edu/thoelogy library/ theology.htm.

4. Fernando Segovia, *Decolonizing Biblical Studies: A View from the Margins* (Maryknoll, NY: Orbis Books, 2000), 155.

5. List or Manifest of Alien Passengers for the United States Migration Office at Port of Arrival, July 8, 1923, *SS Orizaba*, lines 25, Emilio Fernandez, and 26, Carmen G. Fernandez.

6. David Sánchez, *From Patmos to the Barrio: Subverting Imperial Myths* (Minneapolis: Fortress Press, 2008), 124–25.

7. Bonnie J. Miller-McLemore, "Pastoral Theology as Public Theology: Revolutions in the 'Fourth Area,'" in Ramsay, *Pastoral Care and Counseling*, 46.

8. Eldin Villafañe, *The Liberating Spirit: Toward an Hispanic Pentecostal Social Ethic* (Grand Rapids, MI: Eerdmans, 1993), 41, as cited in *Teología en Conjunto: A Collaborative Hispanic Protestant Theology*, ed. José David Rodríguez and Loída Martell-Otero (Louisville, KY: Westminster John Knox Press, 1997), 3.

9. José David Rodríguez and Loída Martell-Otero, "Introduction," in Rodríguez and Martel-Otero, *Teología en Conjunto*, 3.

10. Latino@ theologies are part of a greater stream of scholarship that attends to critical analysis of the daily, including but not limited to some scholars in the areas of feminist theory and culture studies. The explanation for lo cotidiano in this section can also be found in the entry "Lo cotidiano," in *Hispanic American Religious Cultures*, ed. Miguel de la Torre (Santa Barbara, CA: ABC-CLIO, 2009), 158–60.

11. María Pilar Aquino, "Latina Feminist Theologies: Central Features," in *A Reader in Latina Feminist Theology: Religion and Justice*, ed. María Pilar Aquino, Daisy L. Machado, and Jeanette Rodríguez (Austin: University of Texas Press, 2002), 152.

12. María Pilar Aquino, "The Collective 'Discovery of Our Own Power,'" in *Hispanic Latino Theology: Challenge and Promise*, ed. Ada María Isasi-Díaz and Fernando F. Segovia (Minneapolis: Fortress Press, 1996), 256.

13. María Pilar Aquino, "Theological Method in U.S. Latino/a Theology: Toward an Intercultural Theology for the Third Millennium," in *From the Heart of Our People: Latino/a Explorations in Catholic Systematic Theology,* ed. Orlando Espín and Miguel Díaz (Maryknoll, NY: Orbis Books, 1999), 38.

14. Ada María Isasi-Díaz, *Mujerista Theology: A Theology for the Twenty-first Century* (Maryknoll, NY: Orbis Books, 1996), 66–73.

15. Ibid., 66–67.

16. Ibid., 67.

17. Ibid., 68.

18. Orlando Espín, "An Exploration into a Theology of Grace and Sin," in Espín and Díaz, *From the Heart of Our People*, 125.

19. Ibid., 130.

20. Orlando O. Espín, "Traditioning: Culture, Daily Life and Popular Religion, and Their Impact on Christian Tradition," in *Futuring Our Past: Explorations in the Theology of Tradition*, ed. Orlando O. Espín and Gary Macy (Maryknoll, NY: Orbis Books, 2006), 5.

21. Langston Hughes, "Harlem," in *Selected Poems of Langston Hughes* (New York: Random House, 1974), 268.

22. ACHTUS, "Statement Supporting the Passage of the DREAM Act," April 12, 2009. Available on the achtus.org website.

23. ACHTUS, "Statement on Just, Comprehensive, and Humane Immigration Reform," June 7, 2006. Available on the achtus.org website.

24. ACHTUS, "Statement Supporting the Passage of the DREAM Act."

25. USCCB, "Migration Committee Chairman Applauds Introduction of Dream Act, Expresses USCCB Support." Available on the www.usccb.org website.

26. This failure to disseminate the USCCB's stance on the Dream Act was further illustrated at an April 3, 2009, conference at DePaul University in Chicago, appropriately entitled "Bonds of Solidarity: Latinos and Education." Before beginning his plenary address "Education and Respect for Latino Identity," Cardinal Francis George, USCCB president, was compelled to spend the first part of his remarks responding to the Notre Dame matter. The transcript of his text (available on the condor.depaul.edu website) does not reflect this distraction. Unfortunately, the significance of the date in terms of the USCCB support for the DREAM Act, as well as the name and focus of this conference, was lost as media reported only the cardinal's remarks regarding Notre Dame.

27. Miller-McLemore, "Pastoral Theology as Public Theology," 50.

28. Ibid.

29. Richard D. Lamm, "Speakout: Minority Self-Reliance Must Be Stressed Now More Than Ever," *Rocky Mountain News* (February 18, 2006).

30. U.S. Census Bureau, "Income Climbs, Poverty Stabilizes, Uninsured Rate Increases." Available on the census.gov website.

31. "The Hispanic (Latino) Market in the U.S.A.: Generational View," 7th Edition (March 1, 2009). Available online.

32. Nicholas de Genova and Ana Y. Ramos-Zayas, *Latino Crossings: Mexicans, Puerto Ricans, and the Politics of Race and Ctizenship*

(London: Routledge, 2003). Pages 193–210 particularly address issues of class.

33. Ibid., 204.

34. Ibid., 198.

35. Juan Flores, *From Bomba to Hip Hop: Puerto Rican Culture and Latino Identity* (New York: Columbia University Press, 2000), 8.

36. De Genova and Ramos-Zayas, *Latino Crossings*, 197.

37. Pew Hispanic Center, "Changing Faiths: Latinos and Their Transformation of American Religion" (2007), 19. Based on responses to "do you agree/disagree" question no. 52a: "a. God will grant financial success and good health to all believers who have enough faith." According to the study 73 percent of Catholic respondents agreed, 21 percent disagreed; 76 percent of evangelical respondents agreed, 20 percent disagreed. In general there are some problems with this study's rush to label certain responses by Catholics as a result of evidence of the influence of renewalist movements as opposed to evidence of popular religious expressions. Available on the pewforum.org website.

38. Frances R. Aparicio and Susana Chávez-Silverman, "Introduction," in *Tropicalizations: Transcultural Representations of Latinidad* (Hanover, NH: University Press of New England, 1997), 14.

39. Richard Griswold de Castillo, *World War II and Mexican American Civil Rights* (Austin: University of Texas Press, 2008), 98.

40. R. S. Sugirtharajah, *Postcolonial Reconfigurations: An Alternative Way of Reading the Bible and Doing Theology* (London: SCM, 2003), 172.

41. Ibid.

42. Gustavo Gutiérrez, *The Power of the Poor in History: Selected Readings* (London: SCM, 1983), 193.

43. Fernando Segovia, "Towards a Hermeneutics of the Diaspora: A Hermeneutics of Otherness and Engagement," in *Reading from This Place Volume 1: Social Location and Biblical Interpretation in the United States*, ed. Fernando F. Segovia and Mary Ann Tolbert (Minneapolis: Augsburg Fortress Press, 1995), 65.

44. Gustavo Pérez Firmat, *Life on the Hyphen: The Cuban American Way* (Austin: University of Texas Press, 1994), 16.

45. Fernando F. Segovia, "Two Places and No Place on Which to Stand: Mixture and Otherness in Hispanic American Theology," in *Mestizo Christianity: Theology from the Latino Perspective*, ed. Arturo J. Bañuelas (Maryknoll, NY: Orbis Books, 1995), 35.

46. Juana María Rodríguez, *Queer Latinidad: Identity Practices, Discursive Spaces, Sexual Cultures* (New York: New York University Press, 2003), 5.

47. Ed Morales, *Living in Spanglish: The Search for Latino Identity in America* (New York: St. Martin's, 2002), 31.

48. Segovia, *Decolonizing Biblical Studies*, 22.

49. Gary Riebe-Estrella, "Theological Education as *Convivencia,*" in Espín and Díaz, *From the Heart of Our People*, 211–12.

50. Ibid., 212, 213.

## 3. Ortho-proxy and Orthopraxis

1. Fat Joe, Gizmo, Keith Keith, King Sun, "Another Wild Nigga from the Bronx." Lyrics available on the hhdb.com/lyrics website.

2. "Combined Years of Service Total 915 for Retiring USCCB Employees," *America News, Catholic Information and News Service* (February 6, 2007).

3. The first four are "Implementation of the pastoral initiative on marriage; faith formation focused on sacramental practice; priestly and religious vocations; life and dignity of the human person." Available on the usccb.org website.

4. Jerry Filteau, "Bishops Downsize Their National Conference, Reduce Assessments," *Catholic News Service* (November 15, 2006).

5. Ron Cruz, "Message from the Director," *En Marcha* (Fall/Winter 2006). Available on the usccb.org website.

6. USCCB, "Encuentro and Mission: A Renewed Pastoral Framework for Hispanic Ministry," Appendix, no. 69.

7. USCCB, Cultural Diversity in the Church, "Statistics on Hispanic/Latino(a) Catholics." Available on the usccb.org website.

8. David R. Roediger, *Toward the Abolition of Whiteness: Essays on Race, Politics, and Working Class History* (New York: Verso, 1994), 13, as cited in Nicholas De Genova and Ana Y. Ramos-Zayas, *Latino Crossings: Mexicans, Puerto Ricans, and the Politics of Race and Citizenship* (New York: Routledge, 2003), 230n14.

9. R. S. Sugirtharajah, *Postcolonial Reconfigurations: An Alternative Way of Reading the Bible and Doing Theology* (London: SCM Press, 2003), 94.

10. Sean P. O'Connell, *Outspeak: Narrating Identities That Matter* (Albany: State University of New York Press, 2001), 91.

11. Brian K. Blount, *Then the Whisper Put on Flesh: New Testament Ethics in an African American Context* (Nashville: Abingdon Press, 2001), 187.

12. Robert J. Schreiter, *The New Catholicity: Theology Between the Global and the Local* (Maryknoll, NY: Orbis Books, 1997), 4.

13. Jean-Pierre Ruíz, "The Current State of Latina/o Theological Research: A Catholic Perspective. From *We Are a People* to *From the Heart of Our People*," paper presented at Grounding the Next American Century: A National Conference on Funding Latino/a Theological Research, Center for the Study of Popular Catholicism, University of San Diego, February 25–26, 2000, 15, as cited in María Pilar Aquino, "Latina Feminist Theologies: Central Features," in *A Reader in Latina Feminist Theology: Religion and Justice*, ed. María Pilar Aquino, Daisy L. Machado, and Jeanette Rodríguez (Austin: University of Texas Press, 2002), 148.

14. Ada María Isasi-Díaz, *Mujerista Theology: A Theology for the Twenty-first Century* (Maryknoll, NY: Orbis Books, 1996), 6.

15. O'Connell, *Outspeak*, 91.

16. Sharon H. Ringe, "Places at the Table: Feminist and Postcolonial Biblical Interpretation," in *The Postcolonial Bible,* ed. R. S. Sugirtharajah (Sheffield: Sheffield Academic Press, 1998), 139.

17. Dietrich Bonhoeffer, *Life Together* (San Francisco: Harper, 1954), 97.

18. Kenneth Himes, "Globalization's Next Phase," *Origins* (May 23, 2002): 32:2, 21.

19. Jean-Pierre Ruiz, "Reading Between the Lines: Toward a Latino/a (Re)configuration of Scripture and Tradition," in *Futuring Our Past: Explorations in the Theology of Tradition*, ed. Orlando O. Espín and Gary Macy (Maryknoll, NY: Orbis Books, 2006), 83–111.

20. Darien Cavanaugh, "Huelga! Labor Activism and Unrest in Ybor City: 1886–1950," guide to the exhibit at the Ybor City Museum State Park, August 2–October 20, 2003), as cited in Ruiz, "Reading Between the Lines," 87.

21. Ibid.

22. Nancy Hewitt, *Southern Discomfort: Women's Activism in Tampa, Florida, 1880's-1920's* (Urbana: University of Illinois Press, 2001), 273, as cited in Ruiz, "Reading Between the Lines," 88.

23. Ibid.

24. Ibid.

25. Guillermo Gómez-Peña, "The Multicultural Paradigm," *Warrior for Gringostroika*. (St. Paul, MN: Greywolf, 1993), 51, as cited in Frances R. Aparicio and Susana Chávez-Silverman, "Introduction," in *Tropicalizations: Transcultural Representations of* Latinidad (Hanover, NH: University Press of New England, 1997), 5.

26. Gary Riebe-Estrella, "Theological Education Revisited," 2009 Presidential Address, ACHTUS, 3.

27. Ibid., 5.

28. Ringe, "Places at the Table, 137–51.

## 4. The *Imago Dei* in the Vernacular

1. See, for example, Javier Alanis, "The Imago Dei as Embodied in Nepantla, a Latino Perspective," *Currents in Theology and Mission* (December 2005). Available online.

2. See, for example, Virgilio Elizondo, *Galilean Journey: The Mexican-American Promise* (Maryknoll, NY: Orbis Books, 1983); *The Future Is Mestizo: Life Where Cultures Meet* (Oak Park, IL: Meyer-Stone Books, 1988); *Guadalupe, Mother of the New Creation* (Maryknoll, NY: Orbis Books, 1997).

3. See Miguel Díaz, *On Being Human: U.S. Hispanic and Rahnerian Perspectives* (Maryknoll, NY: Orbis Books, 2001).

4. Orlando O. Espín, *Grace and Humanness: Theological Reflections because of Culture* (Maryknoll, NY: Orbis Books, 2007), 65.

5. See Ada María Isasi-Díaz, *En La Lucha, In the Struggle: Elaborating a Mujerista Theology* (Minneapolis: Fortress Press, 1993); *Mujerista Theology: A Theology for the Twenty-first Century* (Maryknoll, NY: Orbis Books, 1996); *La Lucha Continues: Mujerista Theology* (Maryknoll, NY: Orbis Books, 2004).

6. R. S. Sugirtharajah, *Postcolonial Criticism and Biblical Interpretation* (London: Oxford University Press, 2002), 13.

7. Helen Schüngel-Straumann, "On the Creation of Man and Woman in Genesis 1—3: The History and Reception of the Texts Reconsidered," in *Biblical Studies Alternatively: An Introductory Reader*, ed. Susanne Scholz (New York: Prentice Hall, 2002), 80–94, 92–93.

8. Ibid., 93.

9. Juan de Torquemada, *Monarquía Indiana*, bk. 13, chap. 13, pp. 567–68, as cited in Ilona Katzew, *Casta Painting: Images of Race in*

*Eighteenth Century Mexico* (New Haven, CT: Yale University Press, 2004), 47.

10. Guillermo Gómez-Peña, *The New World Border: Prophecies, Poems and Loqueras for the End of the Century* (San Francisco: City Lights, 1996), 26.

11. Quoted in Liliana Obregón, "Rethinking Human Rights, Unshackling the Story," *ReVista: Harvard Review of Latin America* (Fall 2003). Available on the drclas.harvard.edu website. See also John Perry, *Catholics and Slavery: A Compromising History* (Ottawa: Novalis, 2008).

12. Schüngel-Straumann, "On the Creation of Man and Woman in Genesis 1–3," 93.

13. Juana María Rodríguez, *Queer Latinidad: Identity Practices, Discursive Spaces, Sexual Cultures* (New York: New York University Press, 2003), 5.

14. Raúl Gómez Ruiz, *Mozarabs, Hispanics, and the Cross* (Maryknoll, NY: Orbis Books, 2007), 179.

15. See Roberto S. Goizueta, *Caminemos con Jesus: Toward a Hispanic/Latino Theology of Accompaniment* (Maryknoll, NY: Orbis Books, 1995).

16. Gómez Ruiz, *Mozarabs, Hispanics, and the Cross*, 179; and Roberto S. Goizueta, "A Matter of Life and Death: Theological Anthropology between Calvary and Galilee," *Proceedings of the Fifty-third Annual Convention of the Catholic Theological Society of America* 53 (1993): 3–5.

17. Joerg Rieger, *Christ and Empire: From Paul to Postcolonial Times* (Minneapolis: Fortress Press, 2007), 99. Here Rieger draws on Virginia Burrus's understanding of the divine/human natures of Christ as hybrid.

18. William Anthony Nericcio, *Tex{t}-Mex: Seductive Hallucinations of the "Mexican" in America* (Austin: University of Texas Press, 2007), 70.

19. Gómez-Peña, *The New World Border*, 15.

20. See, for example, Maria de Guzmán, *Spain's Long Shadow: The Black Legend, Off-Whiteness, and Anglo-American Empire* (Minneapolis: University of Minnesota Press, 2005). She writes: "Latinas/os claim Spain as an essential component of their own cultural hybridity, but a hybridity in which Spain and Spanishness are not valued over and above any of the other elements and in which Spain is reconceived

in terms of hybridity itself—not merely a static white and/or a Christian Spain, but also an Indo-Afro-Arabic-Jewish one and dynamic, changing even in its own understandings of 'it'-self, that is not culturally monolithic" (302). She comments that philosopher Jorge Gracia also has observed that the Iberian peninsula is inhabited by one of the greatest mixture of peoples in Europe (6).

21. Elizabeth A. Johnson, *Consider Jesus: Waves of Renewal in Christology* (New York: Crossroad, 1990, 2001), 7–8.

22. Peter Brown, *Power and Persuasion in Late Antiquity: Towards a Christian Empire* (Madison: University of Wisconsin Press, 1992), 89.

23. Gregory of Nyssa, *De deitate Filii et Spiritus Sancti*, in *Patrologiae cursus completus (Series Graeca)*, ed. Jacques-Paul Migne (1863), 46:557, as cited in Brown, *Power and Persuasion in Late Antiquity*, 89–90.

24. Rieger, *Christ and Empire*, 91.

25. Interview with Martín Espada, Boston, part of *La Plaza: Conversations with Ilan Stavans,* first aired on PBS-WGBH, September 24, 2002. Available on the martinespada.net website. See also Martín Espada, "Poetry and Politics," *Conversations with Ilan Stavans* (Tucson: University of Arizona Press, 2005), 69–70.

## 5. Handing on Faith en su propia lengua

1. Dame Edna is a drag queen alter ego of Australian comedian Barry Humphries. There was no actual reader's question because the column is intended as comic, tongue-in-cheek satire. Dame Edna, *Vanity Fair* (February 2003), 116. Copies of the text and the Internet petition demanding an apology are available online.

2. "Vanity Fair Apology for Dame Edna Racist Column" (Condé Nast Publications), February 15, 2003. Available online.

3. Juan Gonzalez, *Harvest of Empire: A History of Latinos in America* (New York: Viking Penguin, 2000), 207.

4. Seyla Benhabib, *The Claims of Culture: Equality and Diversity in the Global Era* (Princeton, NJ: Princeton University Press, 2002), 56.

5. In keeping with the accepted practice among Deaf scholars, *deaf* refers to an audiological condition and *Deaf* connotes membership in a community that shares a common language, American Sign Language,

as well as other cultural values, activities, and so forth. In referring to Deaf Latinos/as I use *Deaf* in recognition that communities are created among deaf people who share signed languages other than ASL. In direct quotations I have respected the usage of others. One of the characteristics of theology done latinamente is that it is done en conjunto. I am grateful to the following for their insights and input into this chapter: Min Seo Park, a Deaf Korean who earned his master of divinity degree at St. John's University in New York; Angel Ramos, a Puerto Rican Deaf educator; and Jean-Pierre Ruiz, a Nuyorican biblical scholar.

6. Vilma Santiago-Irizarry, "Deceptive Solidity: Public Signs, Civic Inclusion, and Language Rights in New York City (and Beyond)," in *Mambo Montage: The Latinization of New York*, ed. Agustín Laó-Montes and Arlene Dávila (New York: Columbia University Press, 2001), 474.

7. "A Satire, A Protest, Then an Apology, Satire Is a Dangerous Weapon," *Los Angeles Times*, February 8, 2003. Loosely translated, it means "Angering a bunch of Latinos with laptops can be dangerous."

8. Arlene Dávila, "The Latin Side of Madison Avenue: Marketing and the Language That Makes Us 'Hispanics,'" in Laó-Montes and Dávila, *Mambo Montage*, 411.

9. Ibid., 421–22.

10. Raquel Rivera, "Hip Hop and New York Puerto Ricans," in *Latino/a Popular Culture*, eds. Michelle Habell-Pallán and Mary Romero (New York: New York University Press, 2002), 137–38. See also Raquel Z. Rivera, "Hip-Hop, Puerto Ricans, and Ethnoracial Identities in New York," in Laó-Montes and Dávila, *Mambo Montage*, 248, 256n10.

11. Martín Espada, "The New Bathroom Policy at English High School: Dispatches from the Language Wars," in *Zapata's Disciple: Essays* (Cambridge, MA: South End Press, 1998), 73–74.

12. "There isn't one standardized Spanglish but many. A type of Domincanish is spoken by Dominican Americans in Washington Heights, and it's different from the Pachuco spoken by Mexicans in El Paso and the Cubonics used by Cubans in Union City. And don't forget the ubiquitous cyber-Spanglish, used primarily by webones on the Internet" (Ilan Stavans, "Spanglish Is Everywhere Now, Which Is No Problema for Some, But a Pain in the Cuello for Purists," *Boston Globe*, September 14, 2003).

13. Ilan Stavans, *Spanglish: The Making of a New American Language* (New York: HarperCollins, 2003), 33. Note that Stavans uses the expression "jerga loca" to refer to Spanglish.

14. See Leticia Hernandez-Linares, "'Spanglish' Advancing with Speed and Movida," *Pacific News Service* (March 15, 2001). Available online.

15. Stavans, *Spanglish*, 43.

16. Santiago-Irizarry, "Deceptive Solidity," 474.

17. Benhabib, *The Claims of Culture*, 25–26.

18. Fernando Segovia, "Two Places and No Place on Which to Stand: Mixture and Otherness in Hispanic American Theology," in *Mestizo Christianity: Theology from the Latino Perspective*, ed. Arturo J. Bañuelas (Maryknoll, NY: Orbis Books, 1995), 35.

19. John Leguizamo with David Bar Katz, "Surrogate Moms," in *Freak: A Semi-Demi-Quasi-Pseudo Autobiography* (New York: Riverhead Books, 1997), 53.

20. ASL refers to American Sign Language, a visual-spatial language with its own grammar and syntax used by Deaf people in the United States and in parts of Canada. It is one of the signed languages used in the world by Deaf communities. In the United States, use of ASL is considered a constitutive element in defining Deaf culture.

21. Sign language interpreter Maria Izaguirre interpreted *Freak* in April 1998 for an audience that included 135 Deaf Latin@s. Quoted in "Stars, Musicians, and Jugglers Entertain TKTS Lines As TDF Celebrates Ticket Booth's 25 Years in Duffy Square." Available on the tdf.org website.

22. Gilbert Delgado, "Research Report: Hispanic/Latino Deaf Students in Our Schools," Postsecondary Education Consortium, University of Tennessee (April 2001), 21.

23. Gilbert Delgado, former superintendent of the New Mexico School for the Deaf, quoted in Robert Waddell, "Deaf Latinos Creating Own Support Network" (April 12, 2000).

24. Barbara A. Gerner de Garcia, "ESL Applications for Hispanic Deaf Students," *The Bilingual Research Journal* 19, no. 3–4 (Summer/ Fall 1995), 455.

25. Ibid., 456. Sign languages include, for example, PRSL (Puerto Rican Sign Language), DRSL (Dominican Republic Sign Language), la Lengua de Señas Mexicana, and home signs, that is, "idiosyncratic signs created for communication with family and friends."

26. Tomás García, Jr., "La Promesa de un Tesoro/The Promise of a Treasure" (March 2004).

27. Boris Fridman Mintz, "La realidad bicultural de Sordos e hispanohablantes," Instituto Nacional de Antropología e Historia, September 28, 1999. Available on the cultura-sorda.eu website.

28. Ilan Stavans, "Lexicon: Spanglish>>English," in Stevens, *Spanglish: The Making of a New American Language*, 185.

29. Benhabib, *The Claims of Culture*, 56.

30. Jean-Pierre Ruíz, "Contexts in Conversation: First World and Third World Readings of Job," *Journal of Hispanic/Latino Theology* 2, no. 3 (February 1995): 10.

31. Angel M. Ramos, electronic conversation with this author, November 18, 2003. Ramos is the author of *Triumph of the Spirit: The DPN Chronicle* (Twin Falls, ID: R&R Publishers, 2003). Gallaudet University, in Washington DC, is the only university in the world founded specifically to provide higher education for the Deaf.

32. Douglas Baynton, *Forbidden Signs: American Culture and the Campaign Against Sign Language* (Chicago: University of Chicago Press, 1996), 2.

33. Carol A. Padden, "From the Cultural to the Bicultural: The Modern Deaf Community," in *Cultural and Language Diversity and the Deaf Experience*, ed. Ila Parasnis (Cambridge: Cambridge University Press, 1998), 95.

34. Ibid., 87–88.

35. Ibid., 96.

36. Gerner de Garcia, "ESL Applications for Hispanic Deaf Students," 463.

37. Ibid. The use of the terms *bicultural* and *bilingual* by Deaf scholars is understood in terms of the Deaf and hearing worlds and fluency in ASL and in English in spoken and/or written forms. See Padden, "From the Cultural to the Bicultural: The Modern Deaf Community," 79–98. Multicultural and multilingual reference the increasing transnational and ethnic diversity in the U.S. deaf population as well as recognition of other national languages, sign as well as written and spoken.

38. See Daniel J. Wakin, "Deaf Congregation on East Side Fears for Its Future," The *New York Times*, November 20, 2003. I am grateful to Msgr. Patrick McCahill, pastor of St. Elizabeth of Hungary, the "home" parish for the Catholic Deaf community in the Archdiocese of

New York. Msgr. McCahill patiently taught me sign language during my youth and introduced me to this community, which remains a personal and professional influence in my life.

39. Baynton, *Forbidden Signs*, 150–51. Oralism is used to describe what Deaf culture proponents would label as attempts to assimilate deaf persons by making hearing modalities normative. In education this would include teaching deaf students to speak and lip read and a disparagement of sign language. The battle between oralists and manualists has raged in various forms for more than a century.

40. Susan Burch, "In a Different Voice: Sign Language Preservation and America's Deaf Community," *Bilingual Research Journal* 24, no. 4 (Fall 2000): 339. Residential schools for the Deaf, usually state run, played vital roles in the creation of Deaf senses of community and identity. Remarkably Deaf individuals accomplished this even as many of the institutions sought to eliminate or reduce the use of sign language. In schools, usually in the dormitories, ASL was passed intragenerationally by the Deaf children of Deaf parents to the Deaf children of hearing parents.

41. Baynton, *Forbidden Signs*, 150–51.

42. Robert J. Schreiter, *The New Catholicity: Theology Between the Global and the Local* (Maryknoll, NY: Orbis Books, 1997), 10.

43. Baynton, 154.

44. Katherine A. Jankowski, *Deaf Empowerment: Emergence, Struggle, and Rhetoric* (Washington, DC: Gallaudet University Press, 1997), 89.

45. Ibid., 89–90.

46. Ada María Isasi-Díaz, "A New Mestizaje/Mulatez: Reconceptualizing Difference," in *A Dream Unfinished: Theological Reflections on America from the Margins,* ed. Eleazar Fernandez and Fernando Segovia (Maryknoll, NY: Orbis Books, 2001), 210.

47. R. Greg Emerton, "Marginality, BiCulturalism, Social Identity," in Parasnis, *Cultural and Language Diversity and the Deaf Experience*, 144.

## 6. ¡Cuidado! The Church Who Cares and Pastoral Hostility

1. Martín Espada, *Zapata's Disciples: Essays* (Cambridge, MA: South End Press, 1998), 41.

2. National Conference of Catholic Bishops, Subcommittee on Lay Ministry, *Lay Ecclesial Ministry: The State of the Questions: A Report of the National Conference of Catholic Bishops Subcommittee on Lay Ministry Committee on the Laity* (1999). Available on the usccb.org website.

3. Emmanuel Lartey, "Globalization, Internationalization, and Indigenization of Pastoral Care and Counseling," in *Pastoral Care and Counseling: Redefining the Paradigms*, ed. Nancy J. Ramsay (Nashville, TN: Abingdon Press, 2004), 92.

4. Harold J. Recinos, *Jesus Weeps: Global Encounters on Our Doorstep* (Nashville, TN: Abingdon Press, 1992), 115–31.

5. Ibid., 53.

6. Ada María Isasi-Díaz, *Mujerista Theology: A Theology for the Twenty-first Century* (Maryknoll, NY: Orbis Books, 1996), 71.

7. Orlando Espín, "An Exploration into a Theology of Grace and Sin," in *From the Heart of Our People: Latino/a Explorations in Catholic Systematic Theology*, ed. Orlando Espín and Miguel Díaz (Maryknoll, NY: Orbis Books, 1999), 126.

8. María Pilar Aquino, "Theological Method in US. Latino/a Theology: Toward an Inter-cultural Theology for the Third Millennium," in *From the Heart of Our People*, 39.

9. John Paul II, "Message for the 88th World Day of Migrants and Refugees" (2002), 1. Available on the vatican.va website.

10. Bishop Nicholas A. DiMarzio, "A Welcoming Church: Theory into Practice," in *From Strangers to Neighbors: Reflections on the Pastoral Theology of Human Migration* (Queens, NY: St. John's University Vincentian Center for Church and Society, 2004), 2.

11. Jean-Pierre Ruiz, "Taking the Local: Toward a Contemporary Theology of Migration," in *From Strangers to Neighbors*, 2–18.

12. DiMarzio, "A Welcoming Church," 29.

13. Pontifical Commission for the Pastoral Care of Migrant and Itinerant Peoples, *Letter to Episcopal Conferences on the Church and People on the Move*, May 4, 1978 (Washington DC: United States Catholic Conference, 1978), 12.

14. Ibid., 10.

## 7. Elbows on the Table

1. The empanada is a regional dish of Galicia, Spain. It is made of two bread dough crusts, meat, and onions. The meat and the onions

are sauteed before being placed on the bottom bread dough. The meat may be beef, pork, or chicken, or a combination of all three. Sliced chorizos are added to the meat and onions, and then the top bread dough crust is placed. The empanada may be made in a circular or rectangular pan.

2. Beverly Daniel Tatum, *"Why Are All the Black Kids Sitting Together in the Cafeteria?" And Other Conversations About Race* (New York: Basic Books, 1997), 62.

3. Ada María Isasi-Díaz, "Strangers No Longer," in *Hispanic/ Latino Theology: Challenge and Promise*, ed. Ada María Isasi-Díaz and Fernando F. Segovia (Minneapolis: Fortress Press, 1996), 373–74.

4. María Pilar Aquino, "The Collective 'Discovery' of Our Own Power," in Isasi-Díaz and Segovia, *Hispanic Latino Theology*, 256.

5. Anna Peterson, Manuel Vásquez, and Philip Williams, "The Global and the Local," in *Christianity, Social Change, and Globalization in the Americas,* ed. Anna Peterson, Manuel Vásquez, and Philip Williams (New Brunswick, NJ: Rutgers University Press, 2001), 219.

6. Orlando O. Espín, "Immigration, Territory, and Globalization: Theological Reflections," *Journal of Hispanic/Latino Theology* 7, no. 3 (February 2000): 50.

7. Orlando O. Espín, "La experiencia religiosa en el contexto de la globalización," *Journal of Hispanic/Latino Theology* 7, no. 2 (November 1999): 30.

8. Christopher John Farley, "Introduction: The Beat of Freedom," *Time*, Music Goes Global Special Issue, 158, no. 14 (Fall 2001): 7.

9. Baseball as U.S. civic religion is explored in the anthology *The Faith of Fifty Million: Baseball, Religion, and American Culture*, ed. Christopher H. Evans and William R. Herzog II (Louisville: Westminster John Knox Press, 2002).

10. Robert J. Schreiter, *The New Catholicity: Theology Between the Global and the Local* (Maryknoll, NY: Orbis Books, 1997), 10.

11. Ibid., 10.

12. Pedro Julio Santana (Dominican Republic), quoted in Rob Ruck, *The Tropic of Baseball: Baseball in the Dominican Republic* (Westport, CT: Meckler Publishing, 1991; reprint Lincoln: University of Nebraska Press, 1998), 1–2.

13. Marcos Bretón and José Luis Villegas, *Away Games: The Life and Times of a Latin Baseball Player* (Albuquerque: University of New Mexico Press, 1999), 83.

14. Albert G. Spalding, *America's National Game: Historical Facts Concerning the Beginning, Evolution, Development, and Popularity of Base Ball* (Lincoln: University of Nebraska Press, 1992), 14, cited in Christopher H. Evans, "Baseball as Civil Religion: The Genesis of an American Creation Story," in Evans and Herzog, *The Faith of Fifty Million*, 30.

15. Schreiter, *The New Catholicity*, 12. See also Robert Schreiter, *Constructing Local Theologies* (Maryknoll, NY: Orbis Books, 1985).

16. Roberto González Echevarría, *The Pride of Havana: A History of Cuban Baseball* (London: Oxford University Press, 1999), 187. I borrow the expression "despised but intimate other" from Jean-Pierre Ruiz.

17. Ibid., 133.

18. Manuel Joaquín Báez Vargas, quoted in Rob Ruck, *The Tropic of Baseball: Baseball in the Dominican Republic* (Lincoln and London: University of Nebraska Press, 1998, reprinted from Westport, CT: Meckler Publishing, 1991), 25.

19. Ruck, *The Tropic of Baseball*, 25.

20. González Echevarría, *The Pride of Havana*, 133.

21. Adrián Burgos Jr., "'The Latins from Manhattan': Confronting Race and Building Community in New York City," in *Mambo Montage: The Latinization of New York*, ed. Agustín Laó-Montes and Arlene Dávila (New York: Columbia University Press, 2001), 78.

22. Christopher H. Evans, "The Kingdom of Baseball in America: The Chronicle of an American Theology," in Evans and Herzog, *The Faith of Fifty Million*, 36.

23. Evans, "The Kingdom of Baseball in America," 38–40.

24. Bretón and Villegas, *Away Games*, 94.

25. Richard Lapchick, Alejandra Diaz-Calderon, and Derek McMechan, "The 2009 Racial and Gender Report Card: Major League Baseball," April 15, 2009. Available on the tidesport.org website.

26. David Heim, "Picking Up the Signs," *Christian Century* (December 7, 1994), 1149.

27. Bretón and Villegas, *Away Games*, 14.

28. Jim Caple, "Nobody Wins When the Winners Cheated," ESPN.com: Baseball, August 31, 2001.

29. Danielle Stein, "One Father in Need of Some More Education," *Cornell Daily Sun*, September 5, 2001.

30. Alan M. Klein, *Sugarball: The American Game, the Dominican Dream* (New Haven, CT: Yale University Press, 1991), 59.

31. Ibid., 42.

32. Bretón and Villegas, *Away Games*, 36.

33. Ibid., 35.

34. Ibid., 18.

35. Interview with Alex Rodriguez, March 12, 1996, quoted in Bretón and Villegas, *Away Games*, 39.

36. Bretón and Villegas, *Away Games*, 36.

37. For a detailed discussion of this scandal, see William R. Herzog II, "From Scapegoat to Icon: The Strange Journey of Shoeless Joe Jackson," in Evans and Herzog, *The Faith of Fifty Million*, 97–141.

38. As quoted in Geoffrey Ward and Ken Burns, *Baseball: An Illustrated History* (New York: Knopf, 2000), 142–43. Landis was credited with restoring the public faith in baseball following the 1919 Black Sox scandal. He banned from the sport the eight White Sox players charged with conspiracy to fix the World Series against the Cincinnati Reds, even though the court acquitted the players.

39. Robert Sullivan, "The Bronx Bummer," *Time*, September 10, 2001, 56.

40. "Spring Training Roundup," *Washington Post*, February 16, 2002; "Mets Notebook," *Daily News*, February 22, 2002; Dave Sheinin, "O's Dominican Players Encounter Visa Problems," *Washington Post*, February 23, 2002; Peter Slevin and David Sheinin, "An Age-Old Numbers Game," *Washington Post*, March 2, 2002; David Sheinin, "Rogers and Orioles: Older and Wiser," *Washington Post*, March 8, 2002.

41. "Say It Ain't So, Danny," *USA Today* (August 31, 2001).

42. Peter Slevin and David Sheinin, "An Age-Old Numbers Game," *Washington Post*, March 2, 2002.

43. Bretón and Villegas, *Away Games*, 48.

44. Brian K. Blount, *Then the Whisper Put on Flesh: New Testament Ethics in an African American Context* (Nashville, TN: Abingdon Press, 2001), 40–41.

45. Albert J. Raboteau, *Slave Religion: The "Invisible Institution" in the Antebellum South* (New York: Oxford University Press, 1978), 296. Cited in Blount, *Then the Whisper Put on Flesh*, 41.

46. Blount, *Then the Whisper Put on Flesh*, 41.

47. Adrián Burgos Jr., "'The Latins from Manhattan': Confronting Race and Building Community in New York City," in Laó-Montes and Dávila, *Mambo Montage*, 84.

48. Ibid., 85.
49. Ibid., 84–86 and 77–78.
50. Ibid., 77.
51. Orlando Espín, "An Exploration into a Theology of Grace and Sin," in *From the Heart of Our People: Latino/a Explorations in Catholic Systematic Theology,* ed. Orlando Espín and Miguel Díaz (Maryknoll, NY: Orbis Books, 1999), 126.
52. Burgos, "'The Latins from Manhattan,'" 76.
53. Schreiter, *The New Catholicity,* 10.
54. Sharon H. Ringe, "Places at the Table: Feminist and Postcolonial Biblical Interpretation," in *The Postcolonial Bible,* ed. R. S. Sugirtharajah (Sheffield, UK: Sheffield Academic Press, 1998), 149.
55. Bretón and Villegas, *Away Games,* 245.

## 8. Beyond Hospitality

1. Francisco Alarcón, "Roots/Raíces," in *Laughing Tomatoes and Other Spring Poems/Jitomates Risuenos y otros poemas de primavera* (San Francisco, CA: Children's Book Press, 1997; bilingual edition, 2005), 5.
2. Fernando Segovia, *Decolonizing Biblical Studies: A View from the Margins* (Maryknoll, NY: Orbis Books, 2000), 155.
3. In the spring of 2006 rallies in support of the rights of immigrants in the United States, the white shirt became the visible sign of solidarity, especially for Latin@s. White shirts are typically associated with workers in service industries and agriculture, areas of labor with a high presence of immigrants and Latinos/as. At the June 2006 meeting of the Catholic Theological Society of America (CTSA), white shirts were worn by those members of ACHTUS who also belonged to the CTSA in order to raise awareness and in efforts to have a resolution supporting just immigration reform put on the agenda and passed. The effort was successful. It had been precipitated by a statement on immigration passed earlier in the week by ACHTUS at its annual colloquium (available on the achtus.org website). The text of the CTSA resolution is available on the jcu.edu website.
4. Jean-Pierre Ruiz develops the concept of theology as local in the context of (im)migration in "Taking the Local: Toward a Contemporary Theology of Migration," in *From Strangers to Neighbors: Reflections on the Pastoral Theology of Human Migration* (Queens, NY:

St. John's University Vincentian Center for Church and Society, 2004), 2–18.

5. Alfredo Véa, Jr., *The Silver Cloud Cafe* (New York: Penguin Plume, 1997), 125.

6. Ibid., 198.

7. Gaiutra Bahadur, "The Immigration Debate Then vs. Now: An Old Struggle to Adapt to a New Country's Ways," *The Philadelphia Inquirer*, May 30, 2006.

8. Marilyn Duck, "Bishop Meets with Parishioners Angry over Perceived Slight" (July 26, 2006). Available on the nationalcatholicreporter .org website.

9. Ibid.

10. Ibid.

11. I borrow this expression from Jean-Pierre Ruiz, "Taking the Local."

12. I borrow this expression and image from Donald Pelotte, then bishop of the Catholic Diocese of Gallup, New Mexico, who said: "Not only must your ministries take you to the edge, but you must simultaneously teach the center of society and move the center—sometimes drag the center unwillingly—to the margins where the poor and powerless can be found" (Bishop Donald Pelotte, "Six Challenges for Justice Ministries," *Origins* 21, no. 10 (August 1, 1991), 158.

13. USCCB, "Encuentro and Mission: A Renewed Pastoral Framework for Hispanic Ministry" (2002), no. 73. Available on the usccb.org website.

14. Gastón Espinosa, Virgilio Elizondo, Jesse Miranda, "Hispanic Churches in American Public Life: Summary of Findings," Center for the Study of Latino Religion (Notre Dame, IN: Institute for Latino Studies, University of Notre Dame, January 2003), 17. http:// www.nd.edu/~cslr/research/pubs/HispChurchesEnglishWEB.pdf.

15. Alexandra Stern, *Eugenic Nation: Faults and Frontiers of Better Breeding in Modern America* (Berkeley, CA: University of California Press, 2005), 67. See also the account of the "Bath Riots" in David Dorado Romo, *Ringside Seat to a Revolution: An Underground Cultural History of El Paso and Juarez (1893–1923)* (El Paso, TX: Cinco Puntos Press, 2005), 223–44. For photographic images, see National Museum of American History, Smithsonian Institution, "Opportunity or Exploitation: The Bracero Program," in *America on the Move* online exhibition, americanhistory.si.edu website. For oral histories, see the

Bracero History Archive online at braceroarchive.org. See also *Annual Report of the Surgeon General of the Public Health Service* (Washington DC: Government Printing Office, 1916), available online.

16. Luis Alberto Urrea, *Nobody's Son: Notes from an American Life* (Tucson: University of Arizona Press, 1998), 58.

17. Manuel A. Vásquez, "Historicizing and Materializing the Study of Religion: The Contribution of Migration Studies," in *Immigrant Faiths: Transforming Religious Life in America,* ed. Karen I. Leonard et al. (New York: AltaMira Press, 2005), 238.

18. Fellowship of Reconciliation, Task Force on Latin America and the Caribbean, "The Churches and the Struggle for Peace in Vieques," *Puerto Rico Update* (Spring 2004). Available on the forusa.org website.

19. Ibid.

20. Ibid.

21. Duck, "Bishop Meets with Parishioners Angry over Perceived Slight."

## 9. Justice Crosses the Border

1. Third General Conference of the Latin American Episcopate (CELAM), convened at Puebla, Mexico, January 1979, *Final Document: Evangelization in Latin America's Present and Future*, no. 12, in *Puebla and Beyond*, ed. John Eagleson and Philip Scharper (Maryknoll, NY: Orbis Books, 1979).

2. CELAM, Puebla, *Final Document*, nos. 733, 1134–65.

3. Pope John Paul II, "Communion, Participation, Evangelization," no. 6.9; *Origins* 10, no. 9 (July 31, 1980): 133.

4. María Pilar Aquino, "Theological Method in U.S. Latino/a Theology: Toward an Intercultural Theology for the Third Millennium," in *From the Heart of Our People: Latino/a Explorations in Catholic Systematic Theology,* ed. Orlando O Espín and Miguel H. Díaz (Maryknoll, NY: Orbis Books, 1999), 31.

5. Carmen de Navas-Walt, Bernadette D. Proctor, and Jessica C. Smith, U.S. Census Bureau, *Current Population Reports*, P60–235, "Income, Poverty, and Health Insurance Coverage in the United States: 2007 (Washington DC: U.S. Government Printing Office, 2008), 12. Available on the census.gov website.

6. Kate King, "Hispanic Entrepreneurship, Buying Power on the Rise," CNN, October 1, 2007. Available on the cnn.com website.

7. U.S. Department of Commerce, National Telecommunication and Information Administration (NTIA), and Economics and Statistics Administration (ESA), "Falling through the Net: Toward Digital Inclusion," October 16, 2000. Available on the ntia.doc.gov website.

8. Scarborough Research, "The Power of the Hispanic Consumer Online," 4. Available on the scarborough.com website.

9. Ibid., 13.

10. U.S. Census Bureau, *Current Population Reports*, P60–235, 6.

11. Comment posted April 25, 2009, by Luiggi to column by Esther J. Cepeda, "What Digital Divide? Hispanics Are Online—Now!" *Orlando Sentinel*, posted April 24, 2009. Available on the blogs .orlandosentinel.com website.

12. Dale Russakoff, "Keeping up with the Garcias," *Washington Post*, September 23, 2000.

13. CDF, "Instruction on Certain Aspects of the 'Theology of Liberation,'" *Origins* 14, no. 13 (September 13, 1984): 193, 195–204. Available on the vatican.va website.

14. Bishop James Lyke, O.F.M., "When the Poor Evangelize the Church," *Origins* 10, no. 3 (June 5, 1980): 37.

15. Ibid.

16. Ibid., 36.

17. Ibid.

18. Bishops of Santa Fe Province, "The Southwest's Converging Ethnic Groups," *Origins* 11, no. 39 (March 11, 1982): 623.

19. Ibid., 621–22.

20. Ibid., 622.

21. Ibid., 622–23.

22. Ibid., 623.

23. Ibid.

24. National Conference of Catholic Bishops (NCCB), "The Hispanic Presence: Challenge and Commitment," no. 15; *Origins* 13, no. 32 (January 19, 1984): 539.

25. CDF, "Instruction on Certain Aspects of the 'Theology of Liberation,'" Introduction.

26. Ibid., IX:10.

27. Ibid., IX:9.

28. NCCB, "Catholic Social Teaching and the U.S. Economy," nos. 102–6; *Origins* 14, no. 22–23 (November 15, 1984): 352–53.

29. Ibid., no. 52: 347.

30. John Paul II, "One Church, Many Cultures," nos. 9–10; *Origins* 14, no. 30 (January 10, 1985): 501.

31. NCCB, *Economic Justice for All: Pastoral Letter on Catholic Social Teaching and the U. S. Economy* (Washington DC: United States Catholic Conference, 1986).

32. Paul D. McNelis, S.J., "The Preferential Option for the Poor and the Evolution of Latin American Macroeconomic Orthodoxies," in *The Catholic Challenge to the American Economy: Reflections on the U. S. Bishops' Pastoral Letter on Catholic Social Teaching and the U.S. Economy*, ed. Thomas J. Gannon (New York: Macmillan, 1987), 138.

33. NCCB, *Economic Justice for All,* no. 16.

34. Ibid., no. 90.

35. Ibid., nos. 91–93.

36. Cardinal Joseph Bernardin, "The Fact of Poverty: A Challenge for the Church," *Origins* 14, no. 33 (January 31, 1985): 544.

37. NCCB, *Economic Justice for All,* no. 24.

38. Ibid., no. 120.

39. NCCB, "A Catholic Framework for Economic Life" (November 1996). Available online.

40. "Bishop Skylstad, "Introduction," "Catholic Framework for Economic Life," no. 2. Formerly on the website of the Office for Social Justice, Archdiocese of St. Paul and Minneapolis, osjspm.org.

41. Ibid.

42. NCCB, "Sharing Catholic Social Teaching: Challenges and Directions," *Origins* 28, no. 7 (July 2, 1998): 105. Also available on the usccb.org website.

43. Bernardin, "The Fact of Poverty," 545.

44. CDF, "Instruction on Christian Freedom and Liberation," *Origins* 15, no. 44 (April 17, 1986): 715–28. Also available on the vatican.va website.

45. Bishops of Santa Fe Province, "The Southwest's Converging Ethnic Groups," 622, citing Pope Pius XI, *Quadragesimo Anno*, no. 25.

46. Ibid., 622.

47. NCCB, "The Hispanic Presence," 15, emphasis mine.

48. CELAM, Puebla, *Final Document*, no. 733.

49. CDF, "Instruction on Christian Freedom and Liberation," no. 68.

50. John Paul II, *Centesimus Annus*, no. 57; *Origins* 21, no. 1 (May 15, 1991): 21. Available on the vatican.va website.

51. NCCB, *Economic Justice for All*, no. 88.

52. Bishop John Kinney, "Pastoral Letter on Social Justice Concerns," *Origins* 28, no. 13 (September 10, 1998): 227.

53. Milton Friedman, "Good Ends, Bad Means," in Gannon, *The Catholic Challenge to the American Economy*, 99–100.

54. CELAM, Puebla, *Final Document*, nos. 31–39.

55. John Paul II, "The Priest, the Man of Dialogue," no. 6; *Origins* 12, no. 40 (March 17, 1983): 642.

56. John Paul II, 1984 Christmas message, "The Beatitude of the Poor," no. 8; *Origins* 14, no. 30 (January 10, 1985): 498.

57. Archbishop Rembert Weakland, "The Economic Pastoral and the Signs of the Times," *Origins* 14, no. 24 (November 29, 1984): 394.

58. Allan Figueroa Deck, "The Spirituality of United States Hispanics: An Introductory Essay," *U.S. Catholic Historian* 9, no. 1–2 (Winter 1990): 137–46, as cited in *Mestizo Christianity: Theology from the Latino Perspective*, ed. Arturo Bañuelas (Maryknoll, NY: Orbis Books, 1995), 228.

59. John Paul II, *Sollicitudo Rei Socialis*, no. 38; *Origins* 17, no. 38 (March 3, 1988): 654. Available on vatican.va website.

60. Bishop Ricardo Ramirez, "Poverty in the United States," *Origins* 27, no. 26 (December 11, 1997): 444.

61. John Paul II, *Sollicitudo Rei Socialis*, no. 42.

62. John Paul II, *Centesimus Annus*, no. 28.

63. Ibid., no. 58.

64. Ramirez, "Poverty in the United States," 444.

65. CELAM, Puebla, *Final Document*, nos. 1166–1205.

66. Donal Dorr, *Option for the Poor: A Hundred Years of Catholic Social Teaching* (Maryknoll, NY: Orbis Books, 1983), 394–95n4.

67. CDF, "Instruction on Certain Aspects of the 'Theology of Liberation,'" VI:5.

68. NCCB Secretariat for Hispanic Affairs, "Prophetic Voices: The Document on the Process of the III Encuentro Nacional Hispano de Pastoral," no. 3 (1986), in *Hispanic Ministry: Three Major Documents* (Washington DC: USCC, 1995), 33.

69. NCCB, "Putting Children and Families First: A Challenge for Our Church, Nation and World" (Washington DC: USCC, 1991).

70. CELAM, Puebla, *Final Document*, nos. 1132, 1131.

71. Ibid., no. 1135.

72. Ibid., no. 1174.

73. NCCB, "National Pastoral Plan for Hispanic Ministry," no. 51 (1988), in USCC, *Hispanic Ministry*, 79.

74. Ibid., no. 54.

75. Ibid., no. 56.

76. Ibid., no. 63.

77. María Pilar Aquino, *Our Cry for Life: Feminist Theology from Latin America* (Maryknoll, NY: Orbis Books, 1993), 113.

78. Roberto S. Goizueta, *Caminemos con Jesús: Toward a Hispanic/ Latino Theology of Accompaniment* (Maryknoll, NY: Orbis Books, 1995), 173.

79. Cardinal James Hickey, quoted in *Origins* 14, no. 13 (September 13, 1984): 197.

80. Deck, "Spirituality of United States Hispanics: An Introductory Essay," 228.

81. Roberto Goizueta, "The Preferential Option for the Poor: The CELAM Documents and the NCCB Pastoral Letter on U.S. Hispanics as Sources for U.S. Hispanic Theology," *Journal of Hispanic/Latino Theology* 3, no. 2 (November 1995): 75.

82. DeNeen Brown, "Her Sisters' Keeper," *Washington Post Magazine*, January 23, 2000.

83. Samuel Freedman, "Suburbia Outgrows Its Image in the Arts," *New York Times*, Sunday, February 18, 1999, Arts and Leisure section.

84. Junot Díaz, quoted in ibid.

85. Bishop Donald Pelotte, "Six Challenges for Justice Ministries," *Origins* 21, no. 10 (August 1, 1991): 158.

86. Sylvia Moreno, Philip Pan, and Scott Wilson, "La Nueva Vida/ Latinos in the Washington Region: Established Latinos, Newcomers Perceive Gap," *Washington Post*, January 23, 2000.

87. Ibid.

88. Ibid.

89. John Paul II, *Sollicitudo Rei Socialis*, no. 39.

90. "Summary Report of the Task Force on Catholic Social Teaching and Catholic Education. Available on the usccb.org website.

91. Bishop Kinney, "Pastoral Letter on Social Justice Concerns," 227.

92. Task Force on Catholic Social Teaching and Catholic Education, "Report of the Content Subgroup." Available on the usccb.org website.

93. NCCB, "The Hispanic Presence," 534.

94. William Branigan, "Georgia Town Finds Ways to Cross a Language Barrier," *Washington Post*, February 27, 1999. See Edmund T. Hamann, *The Educational Welcome of Latinos in the New South* (Charlotte, NC: Information Age Publishing, 2008; first published Westport, CT: Praeger Publishers, 2003); and Donald E. Davis, Thomas H. Deaton, David P. Boyle, and JoAnne Schick, eds., *Voices from the Nueva Frontier: Latino Immigration in Dalton, Georgia* (Knoxville: University of Tennessee Press, 2009).

95. Ibid.

96. Moreno, Pan, and Wilson, "La Nueva Vida/Latinos in the Washington Region."

97. Maria Pilar Aquino, "La Mujer/ Women," in *Prophetic Vision. Pastoral Reflections on the National Pastoral Plan for Hispanic Ministry*, ed. Soledad Galerón, Rosa María Icaza, and Rosendo Urrabazo (New York: Sheed and Ward, 1992), 142–62, 316–35.

98. Benedict XVI, *Caritas in Veritate* (June 29, 2009), no. 21. Available on the vatican.va website.

99. George Weigel, "*Caritas in Veritate* in Gold and Red: The Revenge of Justice and Peace (or so they may think)," *National Review Online* (July 7, 2009).

100. Ibid.

101. Benedict XVI, *Caritas in Veritate*, no. 2.

102. Ibid., no. 4.

103. Ibid., no. 58.

104. John Paul II, *Sollicitudo Rei Socialis*, no. 42; *Centesimus Annus*, no. 11.

105. Benedict XVI, *Caritas in Veritate*, no. 2.

106. Ibid., no. 6.

107. Ibid., no. 47.

108. Ibid.

109. Ibid., no. 7.

110. Ibid.

111. Ibid. no. 75.

# Index

183